FOUNDATIONAL TRUTHS

a Modern Catechism

Answering the Essential Questions of Christianity

ISRAEL WAYNE

First printing: December 2023

Master Books, P.O. Box 726, Green Forest, AR 72638

Master Books® is a division of the New Leaf Publishing Group, LLC.

ISBN: 978-1-68344-361-2
ISBN: 978-1-61458-886-3 (digital)
Library of Congress Number: 2023948975

Scripture taken from the King James Version. Public domain. No permission or acknowledgment is required.

All images are from Shutterstock.com.

Please consider requesting that a copy of this volume be purchased by your local library system.

Printed in the United States of America

Please visit our website for other great titles:
www.masterbooks.com

For information regarding promotional opportunities,
please contact the publicity department at pr@nlpg.com.

Master Books®
A Division of New Leaf Publishing Group
www.masterbooks.com

About the Author

Israel Wayne and his wife Brook are homeschooling parents to eleven children.

He is also an author and conference speaker who has a passion for defending the Christian faith and promoting a Biblical worldview. He is the author of *Education: Does God Have an Opinion?*, *Pitchin' A Fit! Overcoming Angry and Stressed-Out Parenting*, *Raising Them Up - Parenting for Christians*, *Answers for Homeschooling - Top 25 Questions Critics Ask*, *Questions God Asks*, *Questions Jesus Asks*, and *Foundations in Faith*.

Since 1995, Israel has traveled the nation speaking on family, homeschooling, revival, discipleship, and cultural issues. He is a frequent guest on national radio and television programs and has been a keynote speaker at numerous conferences. Israel also serves as the Director of Family Renewal, LLC (FamilyRenewal.org) and is the Site Editor for ChristianWorldview.net (a Christian apologetics site).

Table of Contents

How To Use This Book

Take a moment to review how to effectively utilize this book below. *Foundational Truths* is structured into 52 weekly lessons, aiming to equip you to live a deeper life with God every single day. It is versatile and can be used by individuals, families, study groups, and more. The primary goal is to impart the fundamental teachings of God's Word through a question-and-answer format. Each week:

Begin with a Life Question presented on the first two-page spread, such as "Who made God?," "What is Sin?," or "What is the Greatest Commandment?"

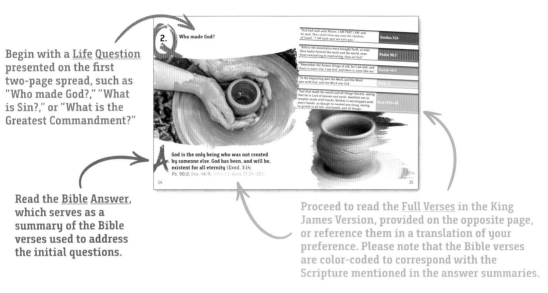

Read the Bible Answer, which serves as a summary of the Bible verses used to address the initial questions.

Proceed to read the Full Verses in the King James Version, provided on the opposite page, or reference them in a translation of your preference. Please note that the Bible verses are color-coded to correspond with the Scripture mentioned in the answer summaries.

Take note of the In Action section, providing guidance on how to apply what you have learned during the week.

A Prayer for This Week is provided to set the tone for the week's focus.

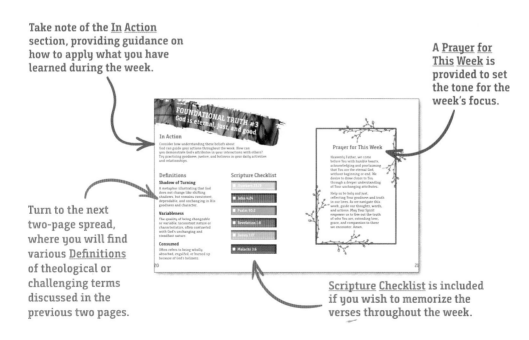

Turn to the next two-page spread, where you will find various Definitions of theological or challenging terms discussed in the previous two pages.

Scripture Checklist is included if you wish to memorize the verses throughout the week.

Introduction

God knows you. He wants you to know Him. Do you? Do you really know Him… and the kind of relationship He wants with you?

Think of this book like a personal Q&A with God. Delve into this modern non-denominational catechism (the part concerning questions and answers about God and the Bible). You'll find some very important things for you to understand in His Word.

Can you give God a few minutes a day? Maybe just a few minutes for:

- Your personal devotion time to restore your faith

- Enrichment of your children's understanding and responsibilities in being a part of God's family

- Giving God a small part of your day to realize His Work in your life

Let's look over a brief history of and foundation for learning to live from God's Word. Let these 52 weekly lessons prepare you to live a deeper life with God every single day.

In our modern church age, the term "catechism" sounds a bit strange and unfamiliar to most of us. What is a catechism, and how can it be useful for your family?

Webster's 1828 Dictionary defines "catechism" this way:

1	A form of instruction by means of questions and answers, particularly in the principles of religion.
2	An elementary book containing a summary of principles in any science or art, but appropriately in religion, reduced to the form of questions and answers, and sometimes with notes, explanations, and references to authorities.

Asking questions can be a wonderful means of teaching.

In ancient Greece, the philosopher Socrates developed a teaching approach that involved asking critical thinking questions to his students that became known as "The Socratic method."

God asked many questions of people in the Bible. Jesus taught His disciples not merely by telling them what they should believe, but by asking them questions. (For more on this, see the books *Questions God Asks* and *Questions Jesus Asks,* by Israel Wayne, published by New Leaf Press.)

What Is Luther's Catechism?

Martin Luther, the founder of the Protestant Reformation, realized that it would be important not only for adults to read the Bible for themselves (in their own language) but for children to learn it as well. In 1529, Luther wrote a catechism for children.

Luther's Large Catechism (also called *Book of Concord 1580*) contained the Ten Commandments, the Apostles' Creed, the Lord's Prayer, the Sacrament of Holy Baptism, the Office of the Keys and Confession, and the Sacrament of the Lord's Table.

What Are Some Other Popular Catechisms?

Here are several historic catechisms that have been used and appreciated by the Christian church since the Protestant Reformation:

(A.D. 1549–1662)	The Anglican Catechism (Church of England)
(A.D. 1563)	The Heidelberg Catechism (Dutch Reformed Church / CRC)
(A.D. 1647)	Westminster Larger Catechism (Presbyterian: 196 questions)
(A.D. 1693)	Benjamin Keach's Catechism (The Baptist Catechism) (118 questions)

What Is the Purpose of a Catechism?

What are the benefits of a catechism? The Anglican (Church of England) Catechism (1549–1662) answers this question for us:

 **What dost thou chiefly learn in these Articles of thy Belief (the creed)?**

 **First, I learn to believe in God the Father, who hath made me, and all the world.**

Secondly, in God the Son, who hath redeemed me, and all mankind.

Thirdly, in God the Holy Ghost, who sanctifieth me, and all the elect people of God.

The purpose of questions provided in any catechism is ultimately to help us to know God. Jesus Himself affirmed this goal as being the most important pursuit of our life:

> "And this is life eternal, that they might know thee the only true God, and Jesus Christ, whom thou hast sent." **John 17:3**

There is no substitute for the Bible. Creeds, confessions, and catechisms are not ever to be a replacement for the Bible. They are simply tools that can help Christians to understand, in a more systematic way, what the Bible teaches. If any of these tools are ever in disagreement with the Bible, they must be set aside in the same way we would dismiss a sermon by our own local church's pastor if it taught something that does not align with the Bible.

Why Do We Need All of These Other Resources? Isn't the Bible Sufficient?

The Bible is all we need for our salvation and our life in Christ. It alone is the living breath of God. But we are blessed today to have many other tools that may be helpful to us in our journey and growth as a Christian. If we do not find these tools to be useful, that's fine. We are not obligated to use them. But often we don't use things like catechisms because we simply don't know they exist or understand their purpose. Our goal in this resource is to point you back to the Word of God directly, in an organized and focused way.

The questions contained in this resource can be memorized if you wish by individuals, students, or by an entire family. You could take one question per week to commit to memory (feel free to shorten answers for young children). It is often helpful to recite the answers together, at least once daily, if you're doing this as a family. This strongly aids in memorizing the answers.

What Bible Translation Is Used in This Book?

For universal application, we chose the King James Version, but feel free to read and/or memorize the verses referenced in this resource in whatever Bible version your family prefers.

1.

How can we know there is a God?

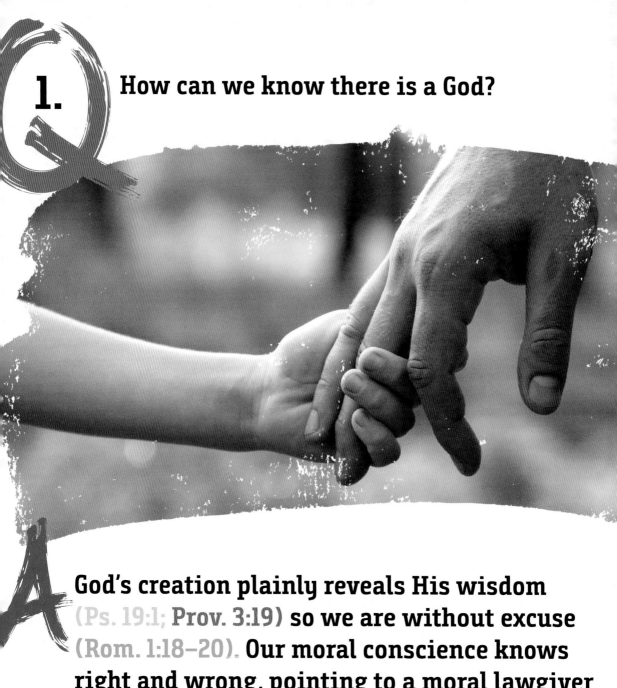

God's creation plainly reveals His wisdom (Ps. 19:1; Prov. 3:19) so we are without excuse (Rom. 1:18–20). Our moral conscience knows right and wrong, pointing to a moral lawgiver (God) (Rom. 2:14–15). The Scriptures are God's Word given to us by God revealing the way of salvation (1 Cor. 1:21–24; 2 Tim. 3:15).

"The heavens declare the glory of God; and the firmament sheweth his handywork."

Psalm 19:1

"The Lᴏʀᴅ by wisdom hath founded the earth; by understanding hath he established the heavens."

Proverbs 3:19

"For the wrath of God is revealed from heaven against all ungodliness and unrighteousness of men, who hold the truth in unrighteousness; Because that which may be known of God is manifest in them; for God hath shewed it unto them. For the invisible things of him from the creation of the world are clearly seen, being understood by the things that are made, even his eternal power and Godhead; so that they are without excuse."

Romans 1:18–20

"For when the Gentiles, which have not the law, do by nature the things contained in the law, these, having not the law, are a law unto themselves: Which shew the work of the law written in their hearts, their conscience also bearing witness, and their thoughts the mean while accusing or else excusing one another."

Romans 2:14–15

"For after that in the wisdom of God the world by wisdom knew not God, it pleased God by the foolishness of preaching to save them that believe. For the Jews require a sign, and the Greeks seek after wisdom: But we preach Christ crucified, unto the Jews a stumbling block, and unto the Greeks foolishness; But unto them which are called, both Jews and Greeks, Christ the power of God, and the wisdom of God."

1 Corinthians 1:21–24

"And that from a child thou hast known the holy scriptures, which are able to make thee wise unto salvation through faith which is in Christ Jesus."

2 Timothy 3:15

FOUNDATIONAL TRUTH #1
We know God through creation and the Scriptures

In Action

Strive this week to make your actions like those desired by God, found in the teachings of the Scriptures.

Each day, identify an opportunity to act in a way that reflects God's wisdom and moral standards. This could involve acts of kindness, forgiveness, love, or seeking justice.

Definitions

Creation

Describes the universe, starting with Earth and all living things made by God in six days. God created the world and everything in it through His divine command, culminating in the creation of humanity in His image.

Unrighteousness

Signifies moral wrongdoing or actions that are opposite of the righteous and just standards set by God, often associated with sin and disobedience to God's commandments.

Wisdom

The ability to apply knowledge, understanding, and discernment in a way that aligns with God's truth and leads to righteous living and a deep relationship with God.

Scripture Checklist

- [ ] Psalm 19:1
- [ ] Proverbs 3:19
- [ ] Romans 1:18–20
- [ ] Romans 2:14–15
- [ ] 1 Corinthians 1:21–24
- [ ] 2 Timothy 3:15

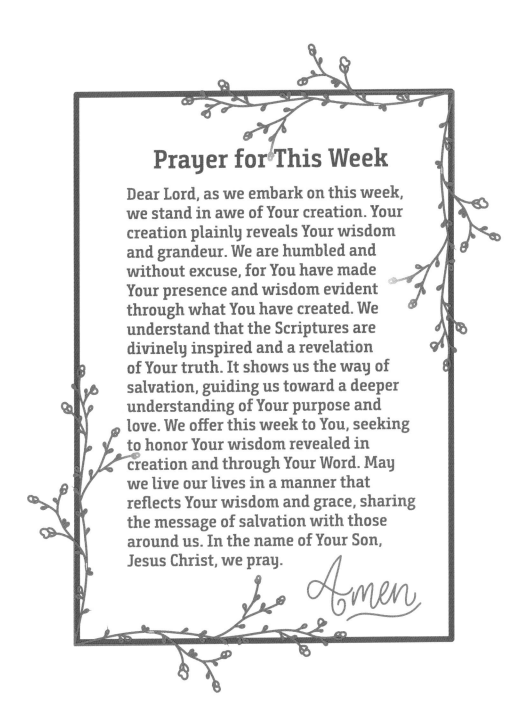

Prayer for This Week

Dear Lord, as we embark on this week, we stand in awe of Your creation. Your creation plainly reveals Your wisdom and grandeur. We are humbled and without excuse, for You have made Your presence and wisdom evident through what You have created. We understand that the Scriptures are divinely inspired and a revelation of Your truth. It shows us the way of salvation, guiding us toward a deeper understanding of Your purpose and love. We offer this week to You, seeking to honor Your wisdom revealed in creation and through Your Word. May we live our lives in a manner that reflects Your wisdom and grace, sharing the message of salvation with those around us. In the name of Your Son, Jesus Christ, we pray.

Amen

2. Who made God?

God is the only being who was not created by someone else. God has been, and will be, existent for all eternity (Exod. 3:14; Ps. 90:2; Isa. 46:9; John 1:1; Acts 17:24–25).

"And God said unto Moses, I AM THAT I AM: and he said, Thus shalt thou say unto the children of Israel, "I AM hath sent me unto you."

Exodus 3:14

"Before the mountains were brought forth, or ever thou hadst formed the earth and the world, even from everlasting to everlasting, thou art God."

Psalm 90:2

"Remember the former things of old: for I am God, and there is none else; I am God, and there is none like me."

Isaiah 46:9

"In the beginning was the Word, and the Word was with God, and the Word was God."

John 1:1

"God that made the world and all things therein, seeing that he is Lord of heaven and earth, dwelleth not in temples made with hands; Neither is worshipped with men's hands, as though he needed any thing, seeing he giveth to all life, and breath, and all things."

Acts 17:24–25

FOUNDATIONAL TRUTH #2
God is everlasting to everlasting

In Action

Set aside time this week to consider incorporating daily prayer and contemplation on the nature of God's eternal existence, expressing gratitude and reverence for this understanding, and seeking to deepen your relationship with God each day.

Definitions

Everlasting

Something that lasts forever or has no end, often used to describe God's attributes or promises.

Existent

Currently exists or has reality or being.

Moses

A biblical figure and prophet who led the Israelites out of Egypt and received the Ten Commandments from God on Mount Sinai.

Scripture Checklist

- ☐ Exodus 3:14
- ☐ Psalm 90:2
- ☐ Isaiah 46:9
- ☐ John 1:1
- ☐ Acts 17:24–25

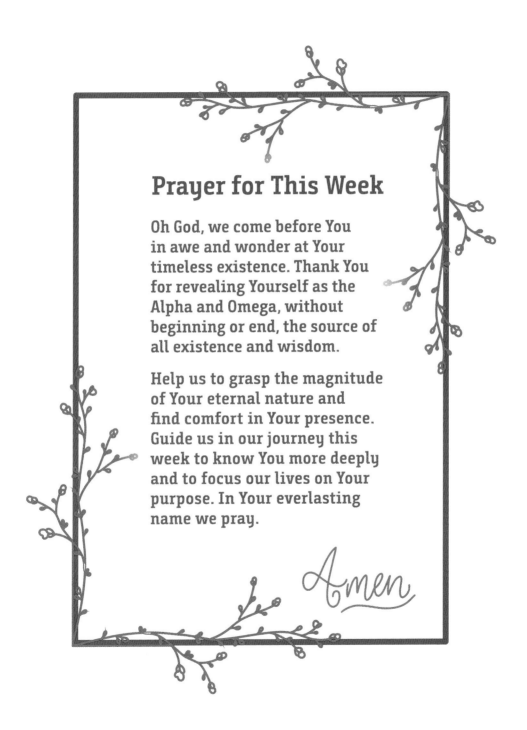

Prayer for This Week

Oh God, we come before You in awe and wonder at Your timeless existence. Thank You for revealing Yourself as the Alpha and Omega, without beginning or end, the source of all existence and wisdom.

Help us to grasp the magnitude of Your eternal nature and find comfort in Your presence. Guide us in our journey this week to know You more deeply and to focus our lives on Your purpose. In Your everlasting name we pray.

Amen

3. Q Who is God?

A God is a Spirit (John 4:24), **without beginning or end** (Ps. 90:2; Rev. 1:8), **unchangeable in His being, wisdom, power, holiness, justice, goodness, and truth** (James 1:17; Mal. 3:6). **There is only one true eternal God: Father, Son, and Spirit.**

"God is not a man, that he should lie; neither the son of man, that he should repent: hath he said, and shall he not do it? or hath he spoken, and shall he not make it good?"

Numbers 23:19

"For I am the LORD, I change not; therefore ye sons of Jacob are not consumed."

Malachi 3:6

"God is a Spirit: and they that worship him must worship him in spirit and in truth."

John 4:24

"Every good gift and every perfect gift is from above, and cometh down from the Father of lights, with whom is no variableness, neither shadow of turning."

James 1:17

"I am Alpha and Omega, the beginning and the ending, saith the Lord, which is, and which was, and which is to come, the Almighty."

Revelation 1:8

FOUNDATIONAL TRUTH #3
God is eternal, just, and good

In Action

Consider how understanding these beliefs about God can guide your actions throughout the week. How can you demonstrate God's attributes in your interactions with others? Try practicing goodness, justice, and holiness in your daily activities and relationships.

Definitions

Shadow of Turning

A metaphor illustrating that God does not change like shifting shadows, but remains consistent, dependable, and unchanging in His goodness and character.

Variableness

The quality of being changeable or variable; inconstant nature or characteristics, often contrasted with God's unchanging and steadfast nature.

Consumed

Often refers to being wholly absorbed, engulfed, or burned up because of God's holiness.

Scripture Checklist

- ☐ Numbers 23:19
- ☐ Malachi 3:6
- ☐ John 4:24
- ☐ James 1:17
- ☐ Revelation 1:8

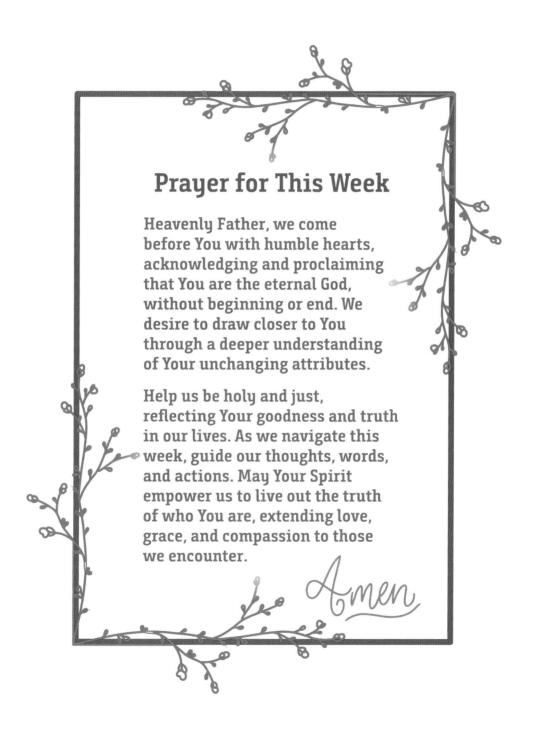

Prayer for This Week

Heavenly Father, we come before You with humble hearts, acknowledging and proclaiming that You are the eternal God, without beginning or end. We desire to draw closer to You through a deeper understanding of Your unchanging attributes.

Help us be holy and just, reflecting Your goodness and truth in our lives. As we navigate this week, guide our thoughts, words, and actions. May Your Spirit empower us to live out the truth of who You are, extending love, grace, and compassion to those we encounter.

Amen

4. How can God be one and yet three persons?

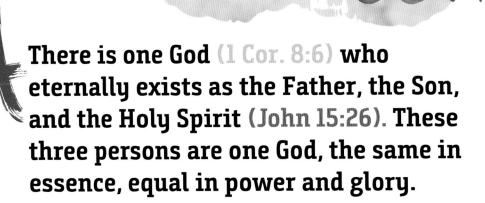

There is one God (1 Cor. 8:6) who eternally exists as the Father, the Son, and the Holy Spirit (John 15:26). These three persons are one God, the same in essence, equal in power and glory.

"The LORD by wisdom hath founded the earth; by understanding hath he established the heavens."

Proverbs 3:19

"Go ye therefore, and teach all nations, baptizing them in the name of the Father, and of the Son, and of the Holy Ghost."

Matthew 28:19

"I and my Father are one."

John 10:30

"Jesus saith unto him, Have I been so long time with you, and yet hast thou not known me, Philip? He that hath seen me hath seen the Father; and how sayest thou then, Shew us the Father?"

John 14:9

"But when the Comforter is come, whom I will send unto you from the Father, even the Spirit of truth, which proceedeth from the Father, he shall testify of me."

John 15:26

"But Peter said, Ananias, why has Satan filled your heart to lie to the Holy Spirit.... thou hast not lied unto men but unto God."

Acts 5:3–4

"But to us there is but one God, the Father, of whom are all things, and we in him; and one Lord Jesus Christ, by whom are all things, and we by him."

1 Corinthians 8:6

"The grace of the Lord Jesus Christ, and the love of God, and the communion of the Holy Ghost, be with you all. Amen."

2 Corinthians 13:14

FOUNDATIONAL TRUTH #4
God is three persons, one in essence

In Action

Dedicate time this week for focused prayer and reflection on the Trinity and consciously apply this understanding in your daily life, living out the belief in one God existing as Father, Son, and Holy Spirit, and reflecting on their unity and equality in power and glory.

Definitions

Baptizing

Water baptism symbolizes the death, burial, and resurrection of our Lord Jesus Christ and the new life found in Him.

Proceedeth

To move forward, continue, or take action in a particular direction or manner.

Essence

The fundamental nature or being of God, comprising Father, Son (Jesus Christ), and Holy Spirit.

Scripture Checklist

- [ ] Proverbs 3:19
- [ ] Matthew 28:19
- [ ] John 10:30
- [ ] John 14:9
- [ ] John 15:26
- [ ] Acts 5:3–4
- [ ] 1 Corinthians 8:6
- [ ] 2 Corinthians 13:14

Prayer for This Week

Thank you, Father, for Your unfailing love, for creating us and guiding our lives. We are grateful that You help provide our homes and food to sustain us. We thank You, Jesus, our Savior and Redeemer, for Your sacrifice and teachings. Holy Spirit, our Comforter and Guide, we welcome Your presence and wisdom.

Help us to grasp the depth of Your unity and embrace the beauty of Your triune nature. May we reflect this unity and love in our lives, treating one another with grace and compassion. In Your name we pray.

Amen

5. **What does God know?**

God knows all things (1 John 3:20): the certain future (Isa. 46:9–11), all possibilities, and even the thoughts (Ps. 139:1–4) and intents of our hearts (John 2:24–25).

"O Lord, thou hast searched me, and known me. Thou knowest my downsitting and mine uprising, thou understandest my thought afar off. Thou compassest my path and my lying down, and art acquainted with all my ways. For there is not a word in my tongue, but, lo, O Lord, thou knowest it altogether."

Psalm 139:1–4

"For God shall bring every work into judgment, with every secret thing, whether it be good, or whether it be evil."

Ecclesiastes 12:14

"Remember the former things of old: for I am God, and there is none else; I am God, and there is none like me, Declaring the end from the beginning, and from ancient times the things that are not yet done, saying, My counsel shall stand, and I will do all my pleasure: Calling a ravenous bird from the east, the man that executeth my counsel from a far country: yea, I have spoken it, I will also bring it to pass; I have purposed it, I will also do it."

Isaiah 46:9–11

"But Jesus did not commit himself unto them, because he knew all men, And needed not that any should testify of man: for he knew what was in man."

John 2:24–25

"Neither is there any creature that is not manifest in his sight: but all things are naked and opened unto the eyes of him with whom we have to do."

Hebrews 4:13

"For if our heart condemn us, God is greater than our heart, and knoweth all things."

1 John 3:20

In Action

Practice surrendering and trusting God's knowledge this week. Keep a journal to jot down your thoughts, concerns, and experiences throughout the week. At the end of each day, write down moments when you felt God's guidance or saw evidence of His knowledge in your life. By consciously acknowledging and surrendering to the fact that God knows all things, and incorporating this awareness into your prayers, reflections, and actions, you can deepen your faith and trust in His wisdom and plan for your life.

Definitions

Condemn

To pronounce judgment or express disapproval of something based on moral or ethical standards, often associated with denouncing sinful actions or behavior.

Compassest

Conveys the idea that God surrounds, understands, and is intimately aware of every aspect of an individual's life.

Testify

To give a personal account or declaration of one's faith, beliefs, experiences, or knowledge.

Scripture Checklist

- [ ] Psalm 139:1–4
- [ ] Ecclesiastes 12:14
- [ ] Isaiah 46:9–11
- [ ] John 2:24–25
- [ ] Hebrews 4:13
- [ ] 1 John 3:20

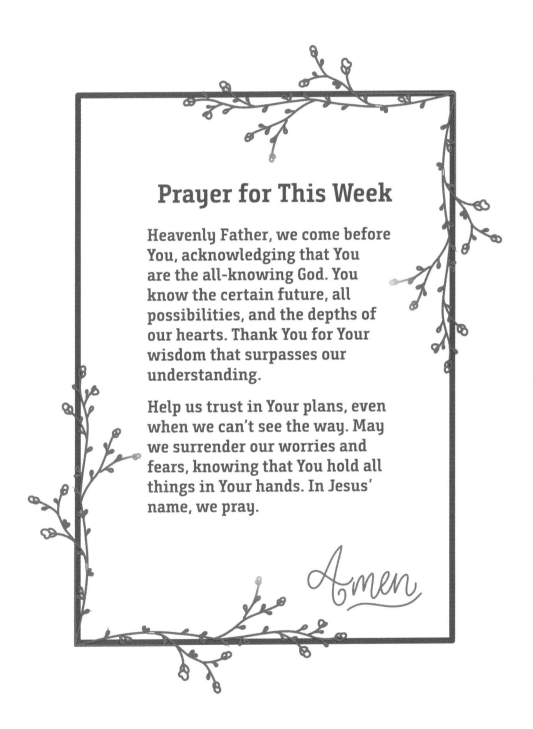

Prayer for This Week

Heavenly Father, we come before You, acknowledging that You are the all-knowing God. You know the certain future, all possibilities, and the depths of our hearts. Thank You for Your wisdom that surpasses our understanding.

Help us trust in Your plans, even when we can't see the way. May we surrender our worries and fears, knowing that You hold all things in Your hands. In Jesus' name, we pray.

Amen

6. Q Are there more gods than one?

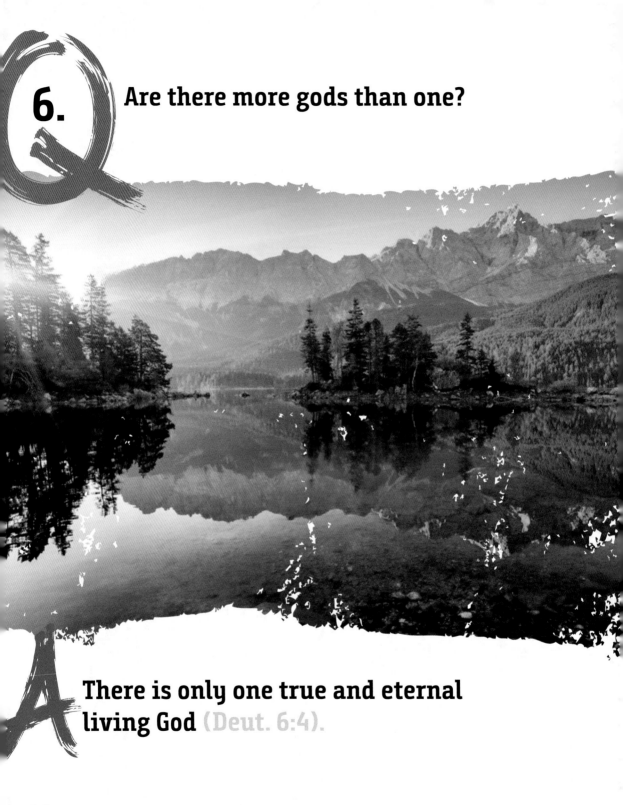

A There is only one true and eternal living God (Deut. 6:4).

"Hear, O Israel: The LORD our God is one LORD."

Deuteronomy 6:4

"But the LORD is the true God, he is the living God, and an everlasting king: at his wrath the earth shall tremble, and the nations shall not be able to abide his indignation."

Jeremiah 10:10

"Ye are my witnesses, saith the LORD, and my servant whom I have chosen: that ye may know and believe me, and understand that I am he: before me there was no God formed, neither shall there be after me."

Isaiah 43:10

"Then remembered I the word of the Lord, how that he said, John indeed baptized with water; but ye shall be baptized with the Holy Ghost."

Acts 11:16

"Yet for us there is but one God, the Father, of whom are all things, and we in him; and one Lord Jesus Christ, by whom are all things, and we by him."

1 Corinthians 8:6

"There is one body, and one Spirit, even as ye are called in one hope of your calling; one Lord, one faith, one baptism, one God and Father of all, who is above all, and through all, and in you all."

Ephesians 4:4–6

FOUNDATIONAL TRUTH #6
There is only one God

In Action

Set aside time each day to read passages from the Bible that emphasize God's nature as the one true and eternal living God (e.g., Psalm 90, Isaiah 40:28–31, Revelation 1:8). Reflect on these verses, pondering the significance of God's eternal existence and sovereignty in your life. Also, reflect on your actions, decisions, and interactions with others throughout the day. Ensure that your actions align with the belief in the one true God, seeking to live a life that reflects His character and teachings.

Definitions

Indignation

A strong feeling of righteous anger or displeasure toward perceived injustice, sin, or wrongdoing, often aligned with God's righteous standards.

Israel

Primarily refers to a nation with significant biblical and prophetic importance. It is the land and people historically associated with the covenant God made with Abraham, Isaac, and Jacob as described in the Bible.

Wrath

The fundamental nature or being of God, comprising Father, Son (Jesus Christ), and Holy Spirit.

Scripture Checklist

- ☐ Deuteronomy 6:4
- ☐ Jeremiah 10:10
- ☐ Isaiah 43:10
- ☐ Acts 11:16
- ☐ 1 Corinthians 8:6
- ☐ Ephesians 4:4–6

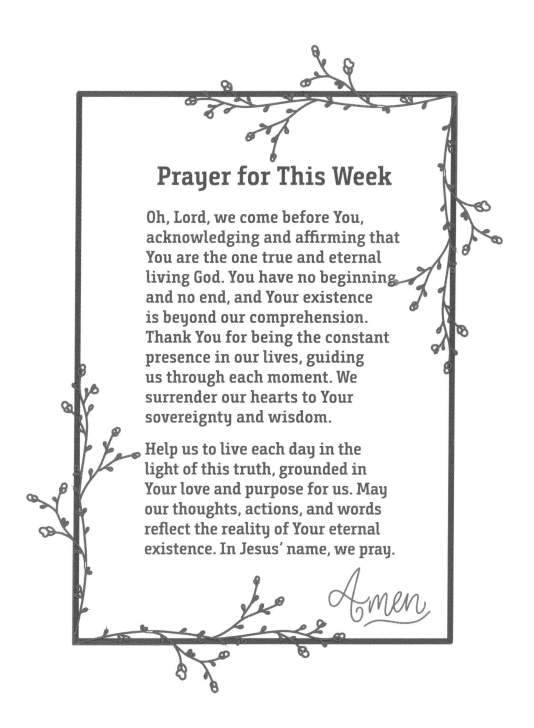

Prayer for This Week

Oh, Lord, we come before You, acknowledging and affirming that You are the one true and eternal living God. You have no beginning and no end, and Your existence is beyond our comprehension. Thank You for being the constant presence in our lives, guiding us through each moment. We surrender our hearts to Your sovereignty and wisdom.

Help us to live each day in the light of this truth, grounded in Your love and purpose for us. May our thoughts, actions, and words reflect the reality of Your eternal existence. In Jesus' name, we pray.

Amen

Q 7. Who created everything?

A God, through His son Jesus Christ (Col. 1:15–17; Heb. 1:2), **created everything that exists** (John 1:1–3): **the visible things and the invisible things** (Col. 1:16).

"And God saw every thing that he had made, and, behold, it was very good. And the evening and the morning were the sixth day."

Genesis 1:31

"In the beginning was the Word, and the Word was with God, and the Word was God. The same was in the beginning with God. All things were made by him; and without him was not any thing made that was made."

John 1:1–3

"[Jesus] is the image of the invisible God, the firstborn of every creature: For by him were all things created, that are in heaven, and that are in earth, visible and invisible, whether they be thrones, or dominions, or principalities, or powers: all things were created by him, and for him: And he is before all things, and by him all things consist."

Colossians 1:15–17

"Hath in these last days spoken unto us by his Son, whom he hath appointed heir of all things, by whom also he made the worlds."

Hebrews 1:2

"Through faith we understand that the worlds were framed by the word of God, so that things which are seen were not made of things which do appear."

Hebrews 11:3

In Action

Take a few moments each day to reflect on the beauty and wonder of creation. Consider the visible things around you — the beauty of nature, the complexity of life, and the intricacies of the universe. Also, contemplate the invisible aspects of creation, such as love, kindness, and the spiritual realm. Offer prayers of gratitude to God for His amazing work of creation.

Definitions

Dominions

Spiritual or celestial authorities and powers, both heavenly and earthly, subject to God.

Principalities

Spiritual beings or realms of authority and power, often associated with spiritual hierarchies and leadership.

Heir

An individual designated to inherit the blessings, promises, and eternal life granted through faith in Christ and adoption into the family of God.

Scripture Checklist

- [ ] Genesis 1:31
- [ ] John 1:1–3
- [ ] Colossians 1:15–17
- [ ] Hebrews 1:2
- [ ] Hebrews 11:3

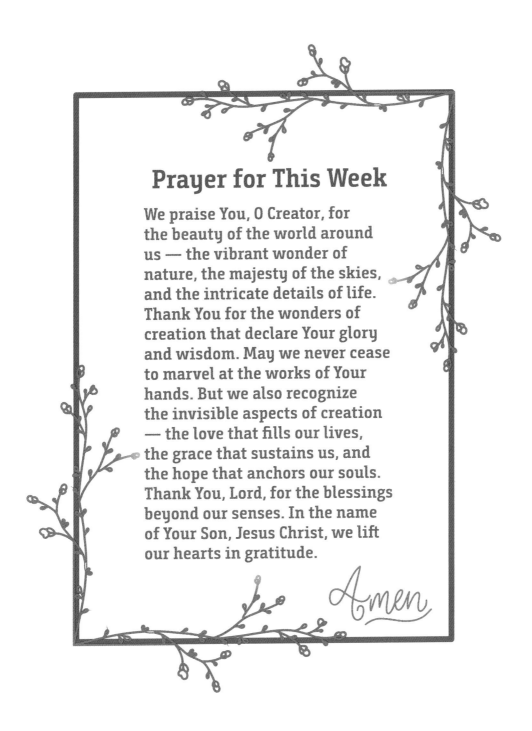

Prayer for This Week

We praise You, O Creator, for the beauty of the world around us — the vibrant wonder of nature, the majesty of the skies, and the intricate details of life. Thank You for the wonders of creation that declare Your glory and wisdom. May we never cease to marvel at the works of Your hands. But we also recognize the invisible aspects of creation — the love that fills our lives, the grace that sustains us, and the hope that anchors our souls. Thank You, Lord, for the blessings beyond our senses. In the name of Your Son, Jesus Christ, we lift our hearts in gratitude.

Amen

8.

Q How did God create all things?

A God created all things by His wisdom (Prov. 3:19), through His spoken command (Gen 1:1–3), in six days.

"In the beginning God created the heaven and the earth.... And God said, Let there be light: and there was light."

Genesis 1:1–3

"O LORD, how manifold are thy works! in wisdom hast thou made them all: the earth is full of thy riches."

Psalm 104:24

"To him that by wisdom made the heavens: for his mercy endureth for ever."

Psalm 136:5

"The LORD by wisdom hath founded the earth; by understanding hath he established the heavens."

Proverbs 3:19

"Ah Lord God! behold, thou hast made the heaven and the earth by thy great power and stretched out arm, and there is nothing too hard for thee:"

Jeremiah 32:17

"All things were made by him; and without him was not any thing made that was made."

John 1:3

"For by him were all things created, that are in heaven, and that are in earth, visible and invisible, whether they be thrones, or dominions, or principalities, or powers: all things were created by him, and for him:"

Colossians 1:16

FOUNDATIONAL TRUTH #8
All was created by God's wisdom and commands

In Action

Take a walk outdoors, preferably in a natural setting like a park, garden, or along a trail. As you walk, observe the beauty of creation around you — the plants, animals, sky, and various elements of nature. Reflect on the intricate design and order that God used in creation. During your walk, pause periodically to reflect on the idea that God spoke creation into being with wisdom and intention. Ponder the wonder of His power and creativity manifested in all that you see and experience.

Definitions

Established

Something firmly set, grounded, or founded on a solid and unchanging foundation.

Manifold

Diverse, abundant, or varied, often used to describe the many aspects, blessings, or attributes of God's grace, wisdom, and goodness that are plentiful and rich in depth.

Mercy

Refers to God's compassion, forgiveness, and lovingkindness toward humanity, particularly in granting undeserved forgiveness and salvation through faith in Jesus Christ, despite our shortcomings and sin.

Scripture Checklist

- [ ] Genesis 1:1–3
- [ ] Psalm 104:24
- [ ] Psalm 136:5
- [ ] Proverbs 3:19
- [ ] Jeremiah 32:17
- [ ] John 1:3
- [ ] Colossians 1:16

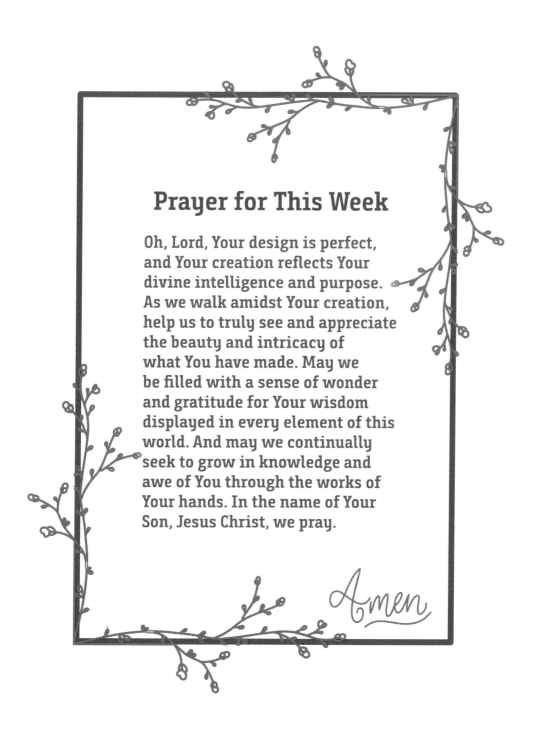

Prayer for This Week

Oh, Lord, Your design is perfect, and Your creation reflects Your divine intelligence and purpose. As we walk amidst Your creation, help us to truly see and appreciate the beauty and intricacy of what You have made. May we be filled with a sense of wonder and gratitude for Your wisdom displayed in every element of this world. And may we continually seek to grow in knowledge and awe of You through the works of Your hands. In the name of Your Son, Jesus Christ, we pray.

Amen

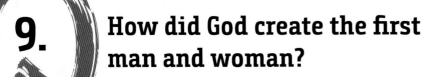

9. How did God create the first man and woman?

God formed Adam from the dust of the ground and breathed into his nose (Gen. 2:7), and he became a living soul. Then God took a rib from Adam's side and fashioned Eve (Gen. 2:21–22).

"And the LORD God formed man of the dust of the ground, and breathed into his nostrils the breath of life; and man became a living soul."

Genesis 2:7

"And the LORD God caused a deep sleep to fall upon Adam, and he slept: and he took one of his ribs, and closed up the flesh instead thereof; And the rib, which the LORD God had taken from man, made he a woman, and brought her unto the man."

Genesis 2:21–22

"Male and female created he them; and blessed them, and called their name Adam, in the day when they were created."

Genesis 5:2

"And (Jesus) answered and said unto them, Have ye not read, that he which made them at the beginning made them male and female?"

Matthew 19:4

"And so it is written, The first man Adam was made a living soul; the last Adam was made a quickening spirit."

1 Corinthians 15:45

"For Adam was first formed, then Eve."

1 Timothy 2:13

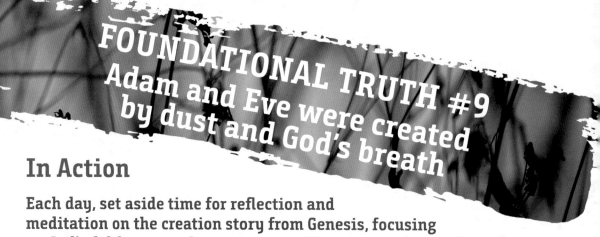

FOUNDATIONAL TRUTH #9
Adam and Eve were created by dust and God's breath

In Action

Each day, set aside time for reflection and meditation on the creation story from Genesis, focusing on God's deliberate and intimate act of forming humanity. Ponder how God's design for relationships is based on mutual respect, love, and support. Throughout the week, strive to embody the principles of kindness, understanding, and compassion in your interactions with others. Seek to cultivate relationships that mirror God's intention for unity and support, just as Adam and Eve were designed to complement each other.

Definitions

Fashioned

To be formed, shaped, or created by God with a specific design, purpose, and intent, often referring to the unique and intentional creation of individuals by God.

Quickening

Refers to the spiritual awakening or enlivening of the soul, often associated with the Holy Spirit's work in bringing spiritual life and vitality to a person, leading to a deeper relationship with God.

Soul

The essential aspect of a person that embodies their consciousness, emotions, and identity, distinct from the physical body, and created to have a relationship with God.

Scripture Checklist

- [ ] Genesis 2:7
- [ ] Genesis 2:21–22
- [ ] Genesis 5:2
- [ ] Matthew 19:4
- [ ] 1 Corinthians 15:45
- [ ] 1 Timothy 2:13

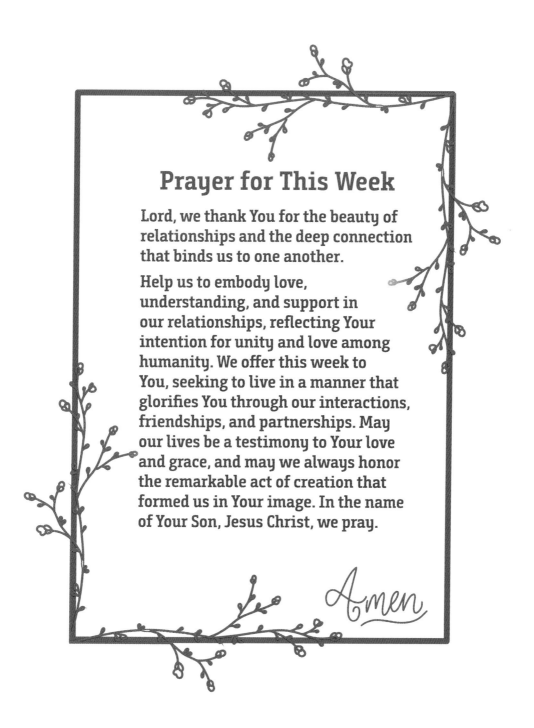

Prayer for This Week

Lord, we thank You for the beauty of relationships and the deep connection that binds us to one another.

Help us to embody love, understanding, and support in our relationships, reflecting Your intention for unity and love among humanity. We offer this week to You, seeking to live in a manner that glorifies You through our interactions, friendships, and partnerships. May our lives be a testimony to Your love and grace, and may we always honor the remarkable act of creation that formed us in Your image. In the name of Your Son, Jesus Christ, we pray.

Amen

10. For what purpose did God create all things?

God created all things for His own glory and pleasure (Eph. 1:9).

"The heavens declare the glory of God; and the firmament sheweth his handywork."

Psalm 19:1

"The LORD hath made all things for himself: yea, even the wicked for the day of evil."

Proverbs 16:4

"Having made known unto us the mystery of his will, according to his good pleasure which he hath purposed in himself."

Ephesians 1:9

"For by him were all things created, that are in heaven, and that are in earth, visible and invisible, whether they be thrones, or dominions, or principalities, or powers: all things were created by him, and for him."

Colossians 1:16

"Thou art worthy, O LORD, to receive glory and honour and power: for thou hast created all things, and for thy pleasure they are and were created."

Revelation 4:11

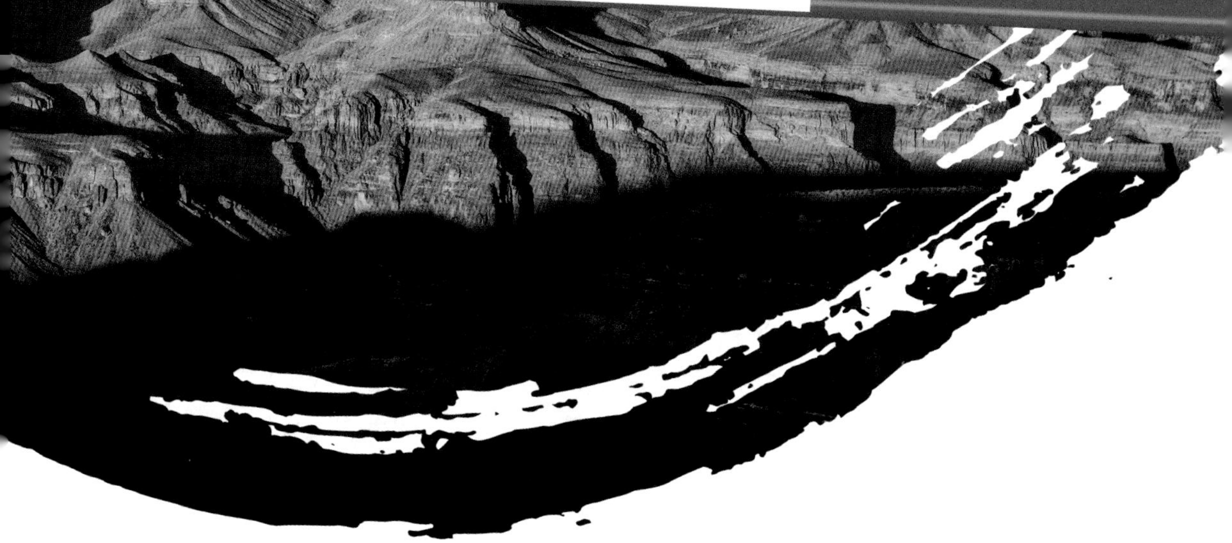

In Action

Integrate moments of praise and worship into your daily routine. Sing hymns, listen to worship music, or spend time in prayer, giving glory and honor to God for His magnificent creation and His love for you. Perform acts of kindness and love toward others, reflecting God's love and compassion. By demonstrating His love to those around you, you showcase God's glory and pleasure in acts of goodness and grace. Take actions to care for and steward God's creation.

Definitions

Firmament

The expanse of the sky or heavens, often described as a solid or firm structure in ancient texts, symbolizing God's creation and sovereignty over the universe.

Glory

Signifies the radiant presence, honor, and magnificence of God. It includes the divine attributes and the splendor that radiates from God's nature and actions, revealing His greatness and beauty.

Mystery

Beyond human comprehension or understanding, often revealed gradually through faith, Scripture, and the Holy Spirit's guidance.

Scripture Checklist

- [ ] Psalm 19:1
- [ ] Proverbs 16:4
- [ ] Ephesians 1:9
- [ ] Colossians 1:16
- [ ] Revelation 4:11

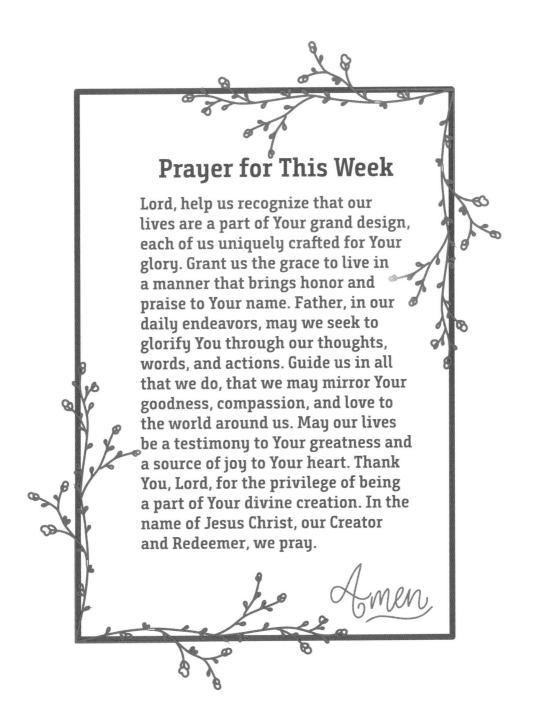

Prayer for This Week

Lord, help us recognize that our lives are a part of Your grand design, each of us uniquely crafted for Your glory. Grant us the grace to live in a manner that brings honor and praise to Your name. Father, in our daily endeavors, may we seek to glorify You through our thoughts, words, and actions. Guide us in all that we do, that we may mirror Your goodness, compassion, and love to the world around us. May our lives be a testimony to Your greatness and a source of joy to Your heart. Thank You, Lord, for the privilege of being a part of Your divine creation. In the name of Jesus Christ, our Creator and Redeemer, we pray.

Amen

11. What is our primary purpose for living?

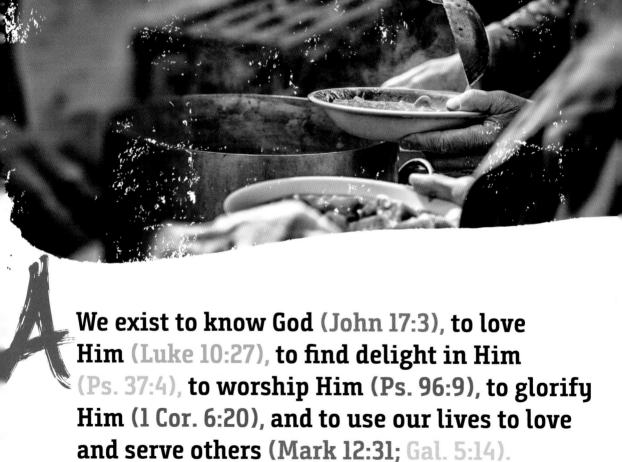

We exist to know God (John 17:3), to love Him (Luke 10:27), to find delight in Him (Ps. 37:4), to worship Him (Ps. 96:9), to glorify Him (1 Cor. 6:20), and to use our lives to love and serve others (Mark 12:31; Gal. 5:14).

"Delight thyself also in the LORD; and he shall give thee the desires of thine heart."

Psalm 37:4

"O worship the LORD in the beauty of holiness: fear before him, all the earth."

Psalm 96:9

"Also I heard the voice of the LORD, saying, Whom shall I send, and who will go for us? Then said I, Here am I; send me."

Isaiah 6:8

"And the second is like, namely this, Thou shalt love thy neighbour as thyself. There is none other commandment greater than these."

Mark 12:31

"And he answering said, Thou shalt love the LORD thy God with all thy heart, and with all thy soul, and with all thy strength, and with all thy mind; and thy neighbour as thyselfe."

Luke 10:27

"And this is life eternal, that they might know thee the only true God, and Jesus Christ, whom thou hast sent."

John 17:3

"For ye are bought with a price: therefore glorify God in your body, and in your spirit, which are God's."

1 Corinthians 6:20

"For all the law is fulfilled in one word, even in this: Thou shalt love thy neighbour as thyself."

Galatians 5:14

In Action

This week, reach out to someone in your community or circle of friends and offer help or support without expecting anything in return. It could be something as simple as checking in on them, offering assistance with a task, or just providing a listening ear. You might also volunteer your time and skills at a local charity, church, or organization that serves those in need. Dedicate a few hours of your week to actively contribute to a cause that aligns with helping others and glorifying God through service.

Scripture Checklist

- ☐ Psalm 37:4
- ☐ Psalm 96:9
- ☐ Isaiah 6:8
- ☐ Mark 12:31
- ☐ Luke 10:27
- ☐ John 17:3
- ☐ 1 Corinthians 6:20
- ☐ Galatians 5:14

Definitions

Commandment

A directive or order given by God in the Bible, intended to guide behavior and demonstrate obedience to God's will.

Glorify

To honor, praise, and acknowledge God's greatness, goodness, and majesty through worship, actions, and words.

Holiness

The state of being set apart, pure, and consecrated to God, characterized by righteous living and devotion to God's commandments.

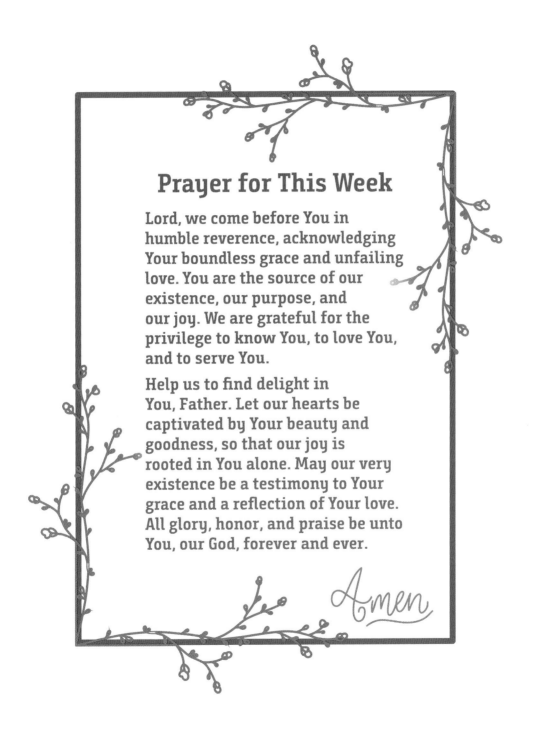

Prayer for This Week

Lord, we come before You in humble reverence, acknowledging Your boundless grace and unfailing love. You are the source of our existence, our purpose, and our joy. We are grateful for the privilege to know You, to love You, and to serve You.

Help us to find delight in You, Father. Let our hearts be captivated by Your beauty and goodness, so that our joy is rooted in You alone. May our very existence be a testimony to Your grace and a reflection of Your love. All glory, honor, and praise be unto You, our God, forever and ever.

Amen

12.

How do we know the 66 books of the Bible are the only inspired Word of God and contain no errors?

The Bible testifies of itself that it is the inspired breath of God (Deut. 29:29; 2 Tim. 3:16; 2 Pet. 1:21). Evidence of its truth includes its unity and consistency (John 17:17), historical accuracy, and life-changing message (Rom. 15:4; Heb. 4:12).

"The secret things belong unto the LORD our God: but those things which are revealed belong unto us and to our children for ever, that we may do all the words of this law."

Deuteronomy 29:29

"Sanctify them through thy truth: thy word is truth."

John 17:17

"For whatsoever things were written aforetime were written for our learning, that we through patience and comfort of the scriptures might have hope."

Romans 15:4

"For this cause also thank we God without ceasing, because, when ye received the word of God which ye heard of us, ye received it not as the word of men, but as it is in truth, the word of God, which effectually worketh also in you that believe."

1 Thessalonians 2:13

"All scripture is given by inspiration of God, and is profitable for doctrine, for reproof, for correction, for instruction in righteousness."

2 Timothy 3:16

"For the word of God is quick, and powerful, and sharper than any twoedged sword, piercing even to the dividing asunder of soul and spirit, and of the joints and marrow, and is a discerner of the thoughts and intents of the heart."

Hebrews 4:12

"For the prophecy came not in old time by the will of man: but holy men of God spake as they were moved by the Holy Ghost."

2 Peter 1:21

In Action

This week, set aside a specific time each day to read and study the Bible. Choose a passage, a chapter, or a particular book to focus on. Reflect on the meaning, context, and message of the text. Identify specific actions or behaviors that align with the teachings of the Bible. Make a conscious effort to live out these principles in your daily life, demonstrating the transformative power of the Word. Apply the life-changing message of the Bible by actively showing kindness, love, and compassion to those around you. Let the teachings of the Bible guide your interactions and responses to others.

Definitions

Inspired

Guided or influenced by the Holy Spirit, often used to describe the process through which the authors of the Bible were divinely guided to write the sacred texts.

Reproof

Gentle or stern criticism, correction, or admonition, often provided with the intention of guiding someone back to a righteous and God-honoring path.

Sanctify

To consecrate or dedicate someone or something to God's service, and to be made holy or pure through the work of the Holy Spirit.

Scripture Checklist

- [ ] Deuteronomy 29:29
- [ ] John 17:17
- [ ] Romans 15:4
- [ ] 1 Thessalonians 2:13
- [ ] 2 Timothy 3:16
- [ ] Hebrews 4:12
- [ ] 2 Peter 1:21

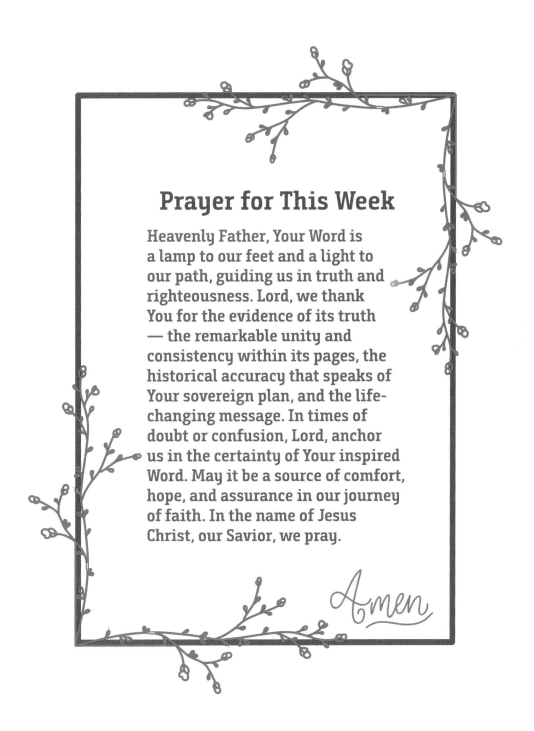

Prayer for This Week

Heavenly Father, Your Word is a lamp to our feet and a light to our path, guiding us in truth and righteousness. Lord, we thank You for the evidence of its truth — the remarkable unity and consistency within its pages, the historical accuracy that speaks of Your sovereign plan, and the life-changing message. In times of doubt or confusion, Lord, anchor us in the certainty of Your inspired Word. May it be a source of comfort, hope, and assurance in our journey of faith. In the name of Jesus Christ, our Savior, we pray.

Amen

13. What is the role of the Holy Spirit in helping us understand the Word of God?

God's Word is confirmed to our hearts by the witness of the Holy Spirit (Ps. 119:18; John 16:13–15; 1 Cor. 2:13–14; 2 Cor. 3:14–16).

"Open thou mine eyes, that I may behold wondrous things out of thy law."

Psalm 119:18

"Howbeit when he, the Spirit of truth, is come, he will guide you into all truth: for he shall not speak of himself; but whatsoever he shall hear, that shall he speak: and he will shew you things to come. He shall glorify me: for he shall receive of mine, and shall shew it unto you. All things that the Father hath are mine: therefore said I, that he shall take of mine, and shall shew it unto you."

John 16:13–15

"Which things also we speak, not in the words which man's wisdom teacheth, but which the Holy Ghost teacheth; comparing spiritual things with spiritual. But the natural man receiveth not the things of the Spirit of God: for they are foolishness unto him: neither can he know them, because they are spiritually discerned."

1 Corinthians 2:13–14

"But their minds were blinded: for until this day remaineth the same vail untaken away in the reading of the old testament; which vail is done away in Christ. But even unto this day, when Moses is read, the vail is upon their heart. Nevertheless when it shall turn to the Lord, the vail shall be taken away."

2 Corinthians 3:14–16

In Action

Set aside a specific time each day this week to read and reflect on a passage from the Bible. As you read, ask the Holy Spirit for guidance and understanding to reveal the deeper meaning and relevance of the Scripture in your life. Spend time in prayer, expressing gratitude for the wisdom and illumination provided by the Holy Spirit and asking for continued guidance and revelation.

Definitions

Confirmed

Validated or affirmed with certainty, often referring to the confirmation of beliefs, truths, or convictions, particularly in matters of faith or spirituality.

Discerned

Perceived, understood, or recognized through careful observation, spiritual insight, or wisdom, often related to distinguishing between right and wrong, truth and deception, or God's will.

Law

Refers to the moral, ethical, and spiritual principles outlined in the Bible that guide believers in living a righteous and God-honoring life.

Scripture Checklist

- [ ] Psalm 119:18
- [ ] John 16:13–15
- [ ] 1 Corinthians 2:13–14
- [ ] 2 Corinthians 3:14–16

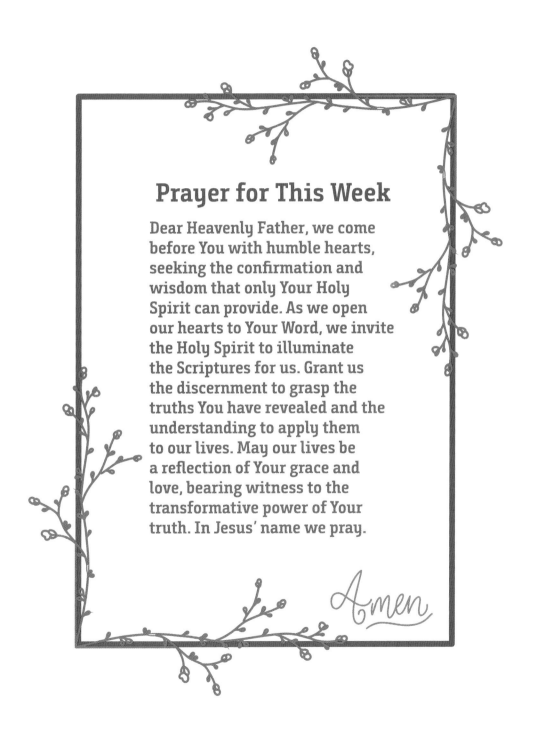

Prayer for This Week

Dear Heavenly Father, we come before You with humble hearts, seeking the confirmation and wisdom that only Your Holy Spirit can provide. As we open our hearts to Your Word, we invite the Holy Spirit to illuminate the Scriptures for us. Grant us the discernment to grasp the truths You have revealed and the understanding to apply them to our lives. May our lives be a reflection of Your grace and love, bearing witness to the transformative power of Your truth. In Jesus' name we pray.

Amen

14. What is the purpose of God's law?

The law was given so we could become aware of our sin (Rom. 3:19–20, 5:20, 7:7) and see our need for a savior (Gal. 3:24–26).

"Now we know that what things soever the law saith, it saith to them who are under the law: that every mouth may be stopped, and all the world may become guilty before God. Therefore by the deeds of the law there shall no flesh be justified in his sight: for by the law is the knowledge of sin."

Romans 3:19–20

"Because the law worketh wrath: for where no law is, there is no transgression."

Romans 4:15

"Moreover the law entered, that the offence might abound. But where sin abounded, grace did much more abound."

Romans 5:20

"What shall we say then? Is the law sin? God forbid. Nay, I had not known sin, but by the law: for I had not known lust, except the law had said, Thou shalt not covet."

Romans 7:7

"For ye are bought with a price: therefore glorify God in your body, and in your spirit, which are God's."

1 Corinthians 6:20

"Wherefore the law was our schoolmaster to bring us unto Christ, that we might be justified by faith. But after that faith is come, we are no longer under a schoolmaster. For ye are all the children of God by faith in Christ Jesus."

Galatians 3:24–26

"For whosoever shall keep the whole law, and yet offend in one point, he is guilty of all. For he that said, Do not commit adultery, said also, Do not kill. Now if thou commit no adultery, yet if thou kill, thou art become a transgressor of the law."

James 2:10–11

In Action

Take an honest inventory of your thoughts, actions, and behaviors throughout the week. Acknowledge and confess your shortcomings and sins to God in prayer, seeking His forgiveness and mercy. Express gratitude for the law's role in helping you recognize your need for redemption and salvation through faith in Christ. Commit to continually seeking a deeper relationship with God, allowing His grace to transform your heart and actions.

Definitions

Flesh

Typically refers to human nature or the physical desires and inclinations that are contrary to God's will.

Guilty

A state of being morally or spiritually responsible for a wrong action, sin, or transgression against God's commandments or teachings as outlined in the Bible.

Transgression

An act of violating a law, command, or moral principle; it signifies crossing a boundary or committing a sin against God's laws.

Scripture Checklist

- [ ] Romans 3:19–20
- [ ] Romans 4:15
- [ ] Romans 5:20
- [ ] Romans 7:7
- [ ] 1 Corinthians 6:20
- [ ] Galatians 3:24–26
- [ ] James 2:10–11

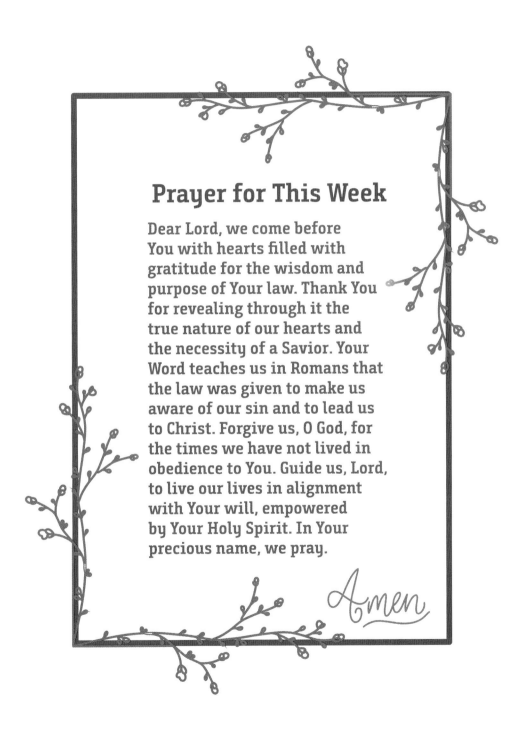

Prayer for This Week

Dear Lord, we come before You with hearts filled with gratitude for the wisdom and purpose of Your law. Thank You for revealing through it the true nature of our hearts and the necessity of a Savior. Your Word teaches us in Romans that the law was given to make us aware of our sin and to lead us to Christ. Forgive us, O God, for the times we have not lived in obedience to You. Guide us, Lord, to live our lives in alignment with Your will, empowered by Your Holy Spirit. In Your precious name, we pray.

Amen

15. What is sin?

Sin is ignoring God, desiring what is contrary to God's law (Matt. 5:22, 28), disobeying God's commands (1 John 3:4), or refusing to obey God's commands (James 4:17).

"But I say unto you, that whosoever is angry with his brother without a cause shall be in danger of the judgment: and whosoever shall say to his brother, Raca, shall be in danger of the council: but whosoever shall say, Thou fool, shall be in danger of hell fire.... But I say unto you, that whosoever looketh on a woman to lust after her hath committed adultery with her already in his heart."

Matthew 5:22, 28

"Because that, when they knew God, they glorified him not as God, neither were thankful; but became vain in their imaginations, and their foolish heart was darkened."

Romans 1:21

"For until the law sin was in the world: but sin is not imputed when there is no law."

Romans 5:13

"Therefore to him that knoweth to do good, and doeth it not, to him it is sin."

James 4:17

"Whosoever committeth sin transgresseth also the law: for sin is the transgression of the law."

1 John 3:4

"All unrighteousness is sin."

1 John 5:17

In Action

Take a few minutes each day to reflect on your actions, thoughts, and desires. Consider if any of these are contrary to what God would want. Confess these areas to God, express genuine remorse (repentance), and ask for His forgiveness. Make a commitment to strive for better alignment with God's will in the coming days. Whenever possible, take steps to correct any wrongs or seek reconciliation with family or friends you may have wronged. Strive to make amends and reconcile with others in a spirit of humility and love.

Definitions

Imputed

The act of attributing or crediting something to someone and is often used to describe how the righteousness of Jesus Christ is credited to believers, making them righteous in the eyes of God.

Raca

Considered an insulting term, expressing contempt or disdain toward someone, this is believed to be an Aramaic term, possibly meaning "empty" or "worthless."

Vain

Being excessively proud or having an exaggerated sense of self-importance, especially when it comes to personal accomplishments or attributes.

Scripture Checklist

- ☐ Matthew 5:22, 28
- ☐ Romans 1:21
- ☐ Romans 5:13
- ☐ James 4:17
- ☐ 1 John 3:4
- ☐ 1 John 5:17

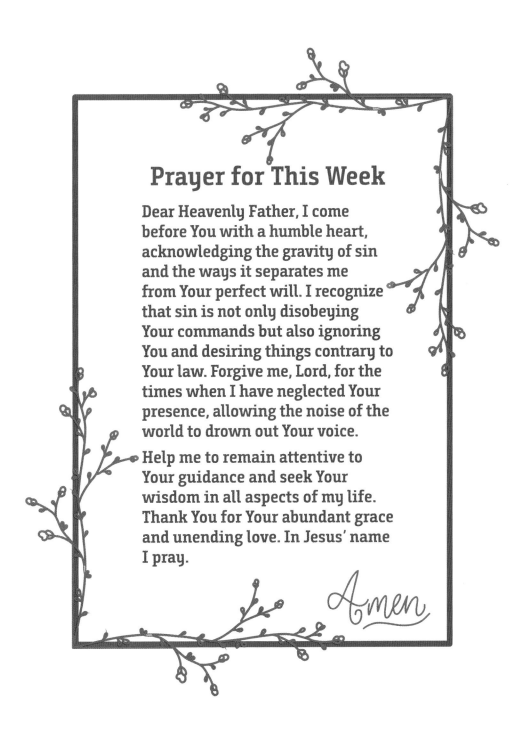

Prayer for This Week

Dear Heavenly Father, I come before You with a humble heart, acknowledging the gravity of sin and the ways it separates me from Your perfect will. I recognize that sin is not only disobeying Your commands but also ignoring You and desiring things contrary to Your law. Forgive me, Lord, for the times when I have neglected Your presence, allowing the noise of the world to drown out Your voice.

Help me to remain attentive to Your guidance and seek Your wisdom in all aspects of my life. Thank You for Your abundant grace and unending love. In Jesus' name I pray.

Amen

16. How did Adam's sin impact the entire world?

Adam's rebellion against God brought all humankind and the entire creation into a state of corruption, disease, death (Rom. 5:12, 8:20–23), **decay, and future judgment** (2 Pet. 3:7, 10).

"And unto Adam he said, Because thou hast hearkened unto the voice of thy wife, and hast eaten of the tree, of which I commanded thee, saying, Thou shalt not eat of it: cursed is the ground for thy sake; in sorrow shalt thou eat of it all the days of thy life; Thorns also and thistles shall it bring forth to thee; and thou shalt eat the herb of the field; In the sweat of thy face shalt thou eat bread, till thou return unto the ground; for out of it wast thou taken: for dust thou art, and unto dust shalt thou return."

Genesis 3:17–19

"Wherefore, as by one man sin entered into the world, and death by sin; and so death passed upon all men, for that all have sinned."

Romans 5:12

"For the creature was made subject to vanity, not willingly, but by reason of him who hath subjected the same in hope, Because the creature itself also shall be delivered from the bondage of corruption into the glorious liberty of the children of God. For we know that the whole creation groaneth and travaileth in pain together until now. And not only they, but ourselves also, which have the firstfruits of the Spirit, even we ourselves groan within ourselves, waiting for the adoption, to wit, the redemption of our body."

Romans 8:20–23

"But the heavens and the earth, which are now, by the same word are kept in store, reserved unto fire against the day of judgment and perdition of ungodly men.... But the day of the Lord will come as a thief in the night; in the which the heavens shall pass away with a great noise, and the elements shall melt with fervent heat, the earth also and the works that are therein shall be burned up."

2 Peter 3:7, 10

In Action

This week, confess your sins to God, seeking His forgiveness and grace to turn away from their destruction. Offer prayers for healing and renewal of both yourself and the world. Pray for those affected by disease and other consequences of sin. Ask God for strength to be a positive influence in a broken world. Throughout the week, actively engage in acts of love, kindness, and service toward others in your home. Take the opportunity to share the message of hope and redemption found in Jesus Christ with someone else. Invite them to understand the consequences of sin and the promise of salvation through faith in Christ.

Definitions

Corruption

The decay, impurity, or moral degradation of individuals, societies, or institutions, moving away from God's intended righteousness and truth.

Fervent

A passionate, heartfelt, and sincere devotion or intensity of spirit in one's faith, prayers, or actions towards God and His purposes.

Travaileth

An older English term that refers to laboring with great effort, striving, or going through intense struggles or hardship, especially in the context of spiritual or emotional struggle.

Scripture Checklist

- [ ] Genesis 3:17–19
- [ ] Romans 5:12
- [ ] Romans 8:20–23
- [ ] 2 Peter 3:7, 10

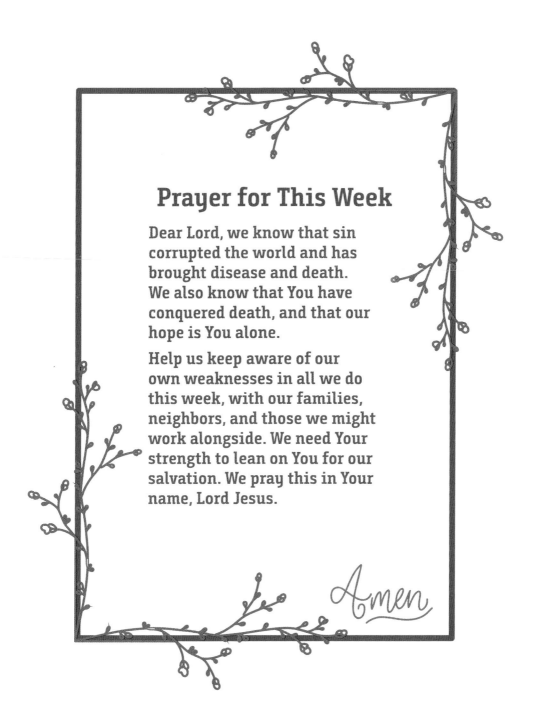

Prayer for This Week

Dear Lord, we know that sin corrupted the world and has brought disease and death. We also know that You have conquered death, and that our hope is You alone.

Help us keep aware of our own weaknesses in all we do this week, with our families, neighbors, and those we might work alongside. We need Your strength to lean on You for our salvation. We pray this in Your name, Lord Jesus.

Amen

17. Have there ever been sinless people?

There has been no one, since Adam and Eve sinned, who was not born with an inclination to willfully sin and rebel against God (Eccles. 7:20), except the Lord Jesus.

"The fool hath said in his heart, There is no God. Corrupt are they, and have done abominable iniquity: there is none that doeth good. God looked down from heaven upon the children of men, to see if there were any that did understand, that did seek God. Every one of them is gone back: they are altogether become filthy; there is none that doeth good, no, not one."

Psalm 53:1–3

"For there is not a just man upon earth, that doeth good, and sinneth not."

Ecclesiastes 7:20

"All we like sheep have gone astray; we have turned every one to his own way; and the LORD hath laid on him the iniquity of us all."

Isaiah 53:6

"What then? are we better than they? No, in no wise: for we have before proved both Jews and Gentiles, that they are all under sin; As it is written, There is none righteous, no, not one: There is none that understandeth, there is none that seeketh after God. They are all gone out of the way, they are together become unprofitable; there is none that doeth good, no, not one."

Romans 3:9–12

"For all have sinned, and come short of the glory of God."

Romans 3:23

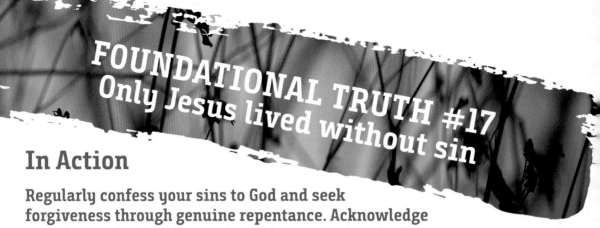

In Action

Regularly confess your sins to God and seek forgiveness through genuine repentance. Acknowledge your innate inclination to sin and express your desire to turn away from it, seeking God's mercy and transformation. Actively engage in acts of service and compassion towards others, modeling the love and grace demonstrated by Jesus. Serve those in need in your own family or community, showing kindness and extending forgiveness, reflecting the character of Christ in your interactions.

Definitions

Corrupt

Morally or spiritually tainted, deviating from righteousness or goodness.

Inclination

A natural tendency or leaning toward a particular action, thought, or behavior.

Iniquity

Immoral or wicked behavior, a violation of God's law or moral principles.

Scripture Checklist

- [ ] Psalm 53:1–3
- [ ] Ecclesiastes 7:20
- [ ] Isaiah 53:6
- [ ] Romans 3:9–12
- [ ] Romans 3:23

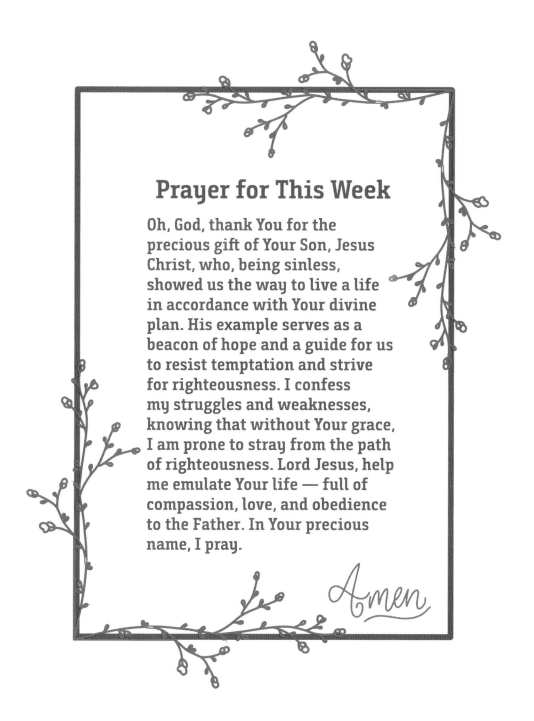

Prayer for This Week

Oh, God, thank You for the precious gift of Your Son, Jesus Christ, who, being sinless, showed us the way to live a life in accordance with Your divine plan. His example serves as a beacon of hope and a guide for us to resist temptation and strive for righteousness. I confess my struggles and weaknesses, knowing that without Your grace, I am prone to stray from the path of righteousness. Lord Jesus, help me emulate Your life — full of compassion, love, and obedience to the Father. In Your precious name, I pray.

Amen

Q **18.** What punishment will those who reject God receive at the judgment?

A The wicked will be eternally separated from God in the lake of fire (Rev. 20:12-15).

"Whose fan is in his hand, and he will thoroughly purge his floor, and gather his wheat into the garner; but he will burn up the chaff with unquenchable fire."

Matthew 3:12

"As therefore the tares are gathered and burned in the fire; so shall it be in the end of this world. The Son of man shall send forth his angels, and they shall gather out of his kingdom all things that offend, and them which do iniquity; And shall cast them into a furnace of fire: there shall be wailing and gnashing of teeth."

Matthew 13:40–42

"And these shall go away into everlasting punishment: but the righteous into life eternal."

Matthew 25:46

"Wherefore, as by one man sin entered into the world, and death by sin; and so death passed upon all men, for that all have sinned."

Romans 5:12

"For we must all appear before the judgment seat of Christ; that every one may receive the things done in his body, according to that he hath done, whether it be good or bad."

2 Corinthians 5:10

"And I saw the dead, small and great, stand before God; and the books were opened: and another book was opened, which is the book of life: and the dead were judged out of those things which were written in the books, according to their works. And the sea gave up the dead which were in it; and death and hell delivered up the dead which were in them: and they were judged every man according to their works. And death and hell were cast into the lake of fire. This is the second death. And whosoever was not found written in the book of life was cast into the lake of fire."

Revelation 20:12–15

In Action

Take the initiative to share the message of salvation and God's grace with someone in your life who may not be familiar with or has not accepted the Christian faith. Communicate the importance of a personal relationship with Jesus Christ as a means to avoid eternal separation from God. Actively display God's love and compassion to others through acts of kindness, empathy, and understanding. Show love to those around you, regardless of their beliefs or actions, mirroring God's desire for all to be saved and experience His grace.

Definitions

Chaff

Worthless or undesirable elements that are separated from the valuable or righteous.

Garner

A place of storage or gathering, symbolizing the gathering of the righteous or believers (represented as wheat) into a place of safety and blessing, while the unrighteous (represented as chaff) will face judgment.

Judgment

The act of determining right from wrong, often associated with God's final evaluation of a person's actions and character.

Scripture Checklist

- [ ] Matthew 3:12
- [ ] Matthew 13:40–42
- [ ] Matthew 25:46
- [ ] Romans 5:12
- [ ] 2 Corinthians 5:10
- [ ] Revelation 20:12–15

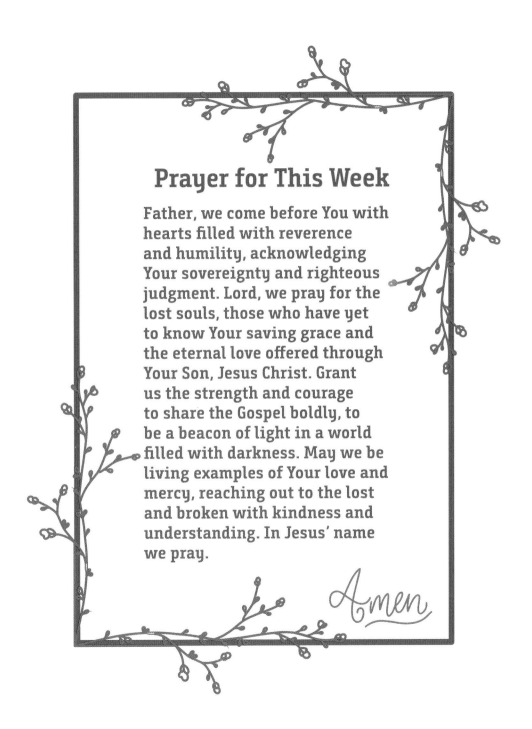

Prayer for This Week

Father, we come before You with hearts filled with reverence and humility, acknowledging Your sovereignty and righteous judgment. Lord, we pray for the lost souls, those who have yet to know Your saving grace and the eternal love offered through Your Son, Jesus Christ. Grant us the strength and courage to share the Gospel boldly, to be a beacon of light in a world filled with darkness. May we be living examples of Your love and mercy, reaching out to the lost and broken with kindness and understanding. In Jesus' name we pray.

Amen

19. Why must God eternally punish sin?

God, who is completely holy and eternal, cannot allow sin (Ps. 5:4–6), which is contrary to His nature (1 John 1:5), to abide in His presence (Hab. 1:13a).

"For thou art not a God that hath pleasure in wickedness: neither shall evil dwell with thee. The foolish shall not stand in thy sight: thou hatest all workers of iniquity. Thou shalt destroy them that speak leasing: the LORD will abhor the bloody and deceitful man."

Psalm 5:4–6

"Thou art of purer eyes than to behold evil, and canst not look on iniquity."

Habakkuk 1:13

"Who shall be punished with everlasting destruction from the presence of the LORD, and from the glory of his power."

2 Thessalonians 1:9

"This then is the message which we have heard of him, and declare to you, that God is light, and in him is no darkness at all."

1 John 1:5

FOUNDATIONAL TRUTH #19
God's nature is complete holiness

In Action

Take a few moments each day to reflect on your actions, thoughts, and attitudes. Consider if there are any behaviors or beliefs that go against God's nature and teachings. If you recognize any sin or contrary actions, sincerely repent and ask for forgiveness. Commit to make amends with anyone you may have hurt, and let your life be a light in the world.

Definitions

Abhor

To strongly dislike or hate something or someone, often due to moral or spiritual reasons.

Contrary

Opposing, going against, or in conflict with a particular belief, principle, or truth.

Destruction

The act or process of causing severe damage, ruin, or the complete breakdown of something.

Scripture Checklist

- ■ Psalm 5:4–6
- ■ Habakkuk 1:13
- ■ 2 Thessalonians 1:9
- ■ 1 John 1:5

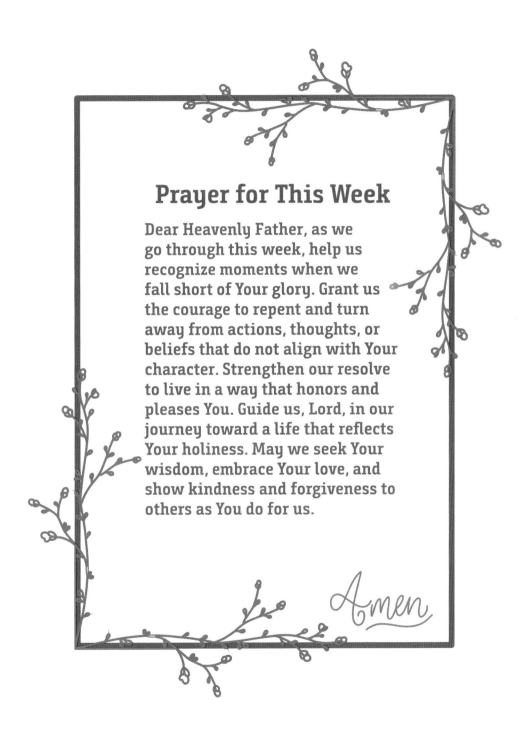

Prayer for This Week

Dear Heavenly Father, as we go through this week, help us recognize moments when we fall short of Your glory. Grant us the courage to repent and turn away from actions, thoughts, or beliefs that do not align with Your character. Strengthen our resolve to live in a way that honors and pleases You. Guide us, Lord, in our journey toward a life that reflects Your holiness. May we seek Your wisdom, embrace Your love, and show kindness and forgiveness to others as You do for us.

Amen

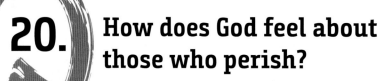

20. How does God feel about those who perish?

God has no pleasure in the death of the wicked (Ezek. 18:23, 32; 33:11), but instead desires all men to come to repentance and be saved (1 Tim. 2:4; 2 Pet. 3:9).

"Have I any pleasure at all that the wicked should die? saith the Lord GOD: and not that he should return from his ways, and live?"

Ezekiel 18:23

"For I have no pleasure in the death of him that dieth, saith the Lord GOD: wherefore turn yourselves, and live ye."

Ezekiel 18:32

"Say unto them, As I live, saith the Lord GOD, I have no pleasure in the death of the wicked; but that the wicked turn from his way and live: turn ye, turn ye from your evil ways; for why will ye die, O house of Israel?"

Ezekiel 33:11

"[Who will] have all men to be saved, and to come unto the knowledge of the truth."

1 Timothy 2:4

"The Lord is not slack concerning his promise, as some men count slackness; but is longsuffering to us-ward, not willing that any should perish, but that all should come to repentance."

2 Peter 3:9

FOUNDATIONAL TRUTH #20
God wants all people saved

In Action

Throughout this week, make an effort to show love, understanding, and kindness to everyone you encounter. Reach out to someone you may have had disagreements with or someone who might be distant. Be open to listening and understanding their perspective without judgment. Share a genuine smile, offer a word of encouragement, or lend a helping hand to someone in need. Let your actions reflect God's desire for all to come to repentance and experience His love.

Definitions

Longsuffering

Patience, endurance, and forbearance in the face of difficult circumstances or the slowness of others to change or repent.

Repentance

The act of acknowledging one's sins or wrongdoings, feeling genuine remorse, seeking forgiveness, and committing to turn away from those actions in order to align with God's will.

Slack

A state of spiritual indifference, negligence, or a lack of effort in pursuing one's faith or responsibilities.

Scripture Checklist

- ☐ Ezekiel 18:23
- ☐ Ezekiel 18:32
- ☐ Ezekiel 33:11
- ☐ 1 Timothy 2:4
- ☐ 2 Peter 3:9

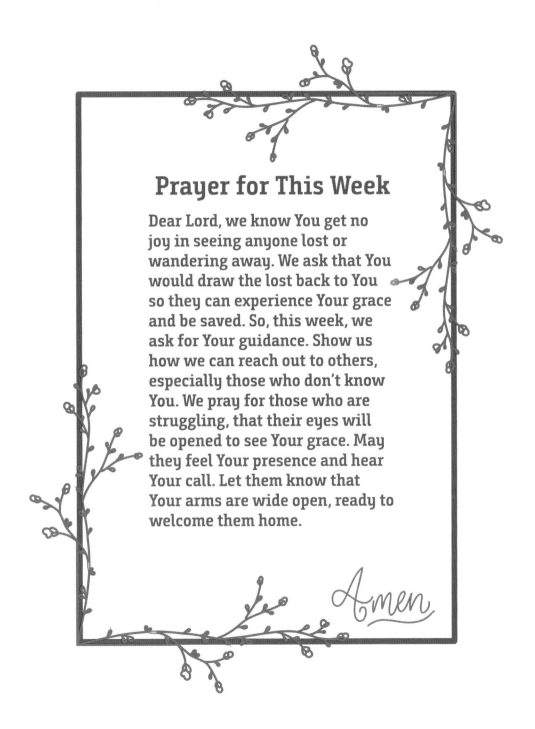

Prayer for This Week

Dear Lord, we know You get no joy in seeing anyone lost or wandering away. We ask that You would draw the lost back to You so they can experience Your grace and be saved. So, this week, we ask for Your guidance. Show us how we can reach out to others, especially those who don't know You. We pray for those who are struggling, that their eyes will be opened to see Your grace. May they feel Your presence and hear Your call. Let them know that Your arms are wide open, ready to welcome them home.

Amen

21. How do we know Jesus is God's only begotten Son?

God the Father spoke from Heaven, at Jesus' baptism (Matt. 3:17) and transfiguration (Matt. 17:5), declaring Jesus to be His only begotten Son.

"And, lo, a voice from heaven, saying, This is my beloved Son, in whom I am well pleased."

Matthew 3:17

"While he yet spake, behold, a bright cloud overshadowed them: and behold a voice out of the cloud, which said, This is my beloved Son, in whom I am well pleased; hear ye him."

Matthew 17:5

"And the Word was made flesh, and dwelt among us, (and we beheld his glory, the glory as of the only begotten of the Father), full of grace and truth.... No man hath seen God at any time, the only begotten Son, which is in the bosom of the Father, he hath declared him."

John 1:14, 18

"For God so loved the world, that he gave his only begotten Son, that whosoever believeth in him should not perish, but have everlasting life."

John 3:16

"And we know that the Son of God is come, and hath given us an understanding, that we may know him that is true, and we are in him that is true, even in his Son Jesus Christ. This is the true God, and eternal life."

1 John 5:20

In Action

Take a few moments during the week to reflect on your faith and relationship with Jesus Christ. Just like God declared Jesus as His beloved Son, affirm your belief in Jesus as the Son of God and the Savior of your life. Remind yourself of the significance of Jesus' baptism and transfiguration in affirming His divine nature and purpose. You can do this through a brief prayer, journaling, or simply having a quiet moment of reflection.

Definitions

Begotten

Jesus is often referred to as the "only begotten Son of God," emphasizing His divine and eternal nature.

Grace

The unmerited favor and love of God toward humanity. It is a gift from God that brings salvation and enables believers to live a life in accordance with God's will.

Transfiguration

The event described in the Gospels where Jesus underwent a divine and radiant transformation in the presence of His disciples, revealing the glorified state of Christ.

Scripture Checklist

- [ ] Matthew 3:17
- [ ] Matthew 17:5
- [ ] John 1:14, 18
- [ ] John 3:16
- [ ] 1 John 5:20

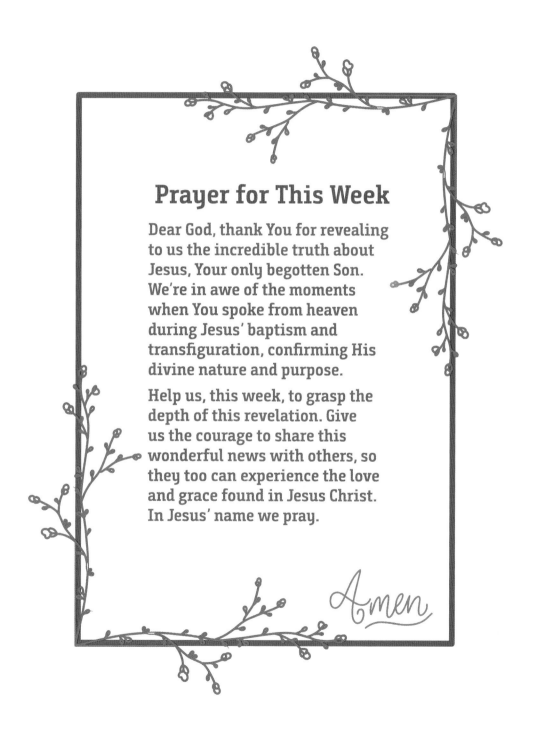

Prayer for This Week

Dear God, thank You for revealing to us the incredible truth about Jesus, Your only begotten Son. We're in awe of the moments when You spoke from heaven during Jesus' baptism and transfiguration, confirming His divine nature and purpose.

Help us, this week, to grasp the depth of this revelation. Give us the courage to share this wonderful news with others, so they too can experience the love and grace found in Jesus Christ. In Jesus' name we pray.

Amen

22. Why is Jesus called God's "only begotten Son" when true believers also are God's children?

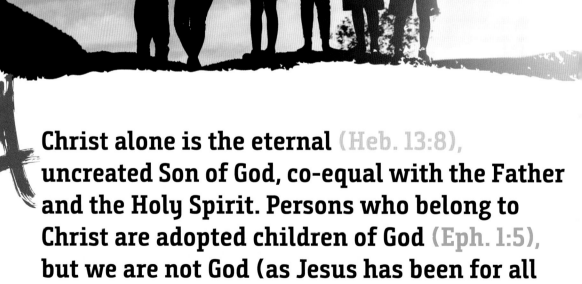

Christ alone is the eternal (Heb. 13:8), uncreated Son of God, co-equal with the Father and the Holy Spirit. Persons who belong to Christ are adopted children of God (Eph. 1:5), but we are not God (as Jesus has been for all eternity), nor can we ever become "gods."

"... who hath told it from that time? have not I the LORD? And there is no God else beside me; a just God and a Saviour; there is none beside me."

Isaiah 45:21

"Have we not all one father? hath not one God created us?"

Malachi 2:10

"And Jesus answered him, The first of all the commandments is, Hear, O Israel: The Lord our God is one Lord."

Mark 12:29

"God hath fulfilled the same unto us their children, in that he hath raised up Jesus again; as it is also written in the second psalm, Thou art my Son, this day have I begotten thee."

Acts 13:33

"For ye have not received the spirit of bondage again to fear; but ye have received the Spirit of adoption, whereby we cry, Abba, Father."

Romans 8:15

"But to us there is but one God, the Father, of whom are all things, and we in him; and one Lord Jesus Christ, by whom are all things, and we by him."

1 Corinthians 8:6

"Having predestinated us unto the adoption of children by Jesus Christ to himself, according to the good pleasure of his will."

Ephesians 1:5

"For unto which of the angels said he at any time, Thou art my Son, this day have I begotten thee? And again, I will be to him a Father, and he shall be to me a Son?"

Hebrews 1:5

"Jesus Christ the same yesterday, and to day, and for ever."

Hebrews 13:8

In Action

Take a few moments during the week to reflect on your faith and relationship with Jesus Christ. Affirm your belief in Jesus as the Son of God and the Savior of your life. Remind yourself of the significance of Jesus' baptism and transfiguration in affirming His divine nature and purpose. You can do this through a brief prayer, journaling, or simply having a quiet moment of reflection.

Definitions

Abba

An Aramaic word used in the New Testament, particularly by Jesus, to address God the Father in an intimate and affectionate manner.

Adoption

Speaks of the spiritual concept of believers being chosen and welcomed into God's family as His children through faith in Jesus Christ.

Predestinated

The belief that God has foreordained a plan for His elect believers to be conformed into the image of Jesus Christ.

Scripture Checklist

- [ ] Isaiah 45:21
- [ ] Malachi 2:10
- [ ] Mark 12:29
- [ ] Acts 13:33
- [ ] Romans 8:15
- [ ] 1 Corinthians 8:6
- [ ] Ephesians 1:5
- [ ] Hebrews 1:5
- [ ] Hebrews 13:8

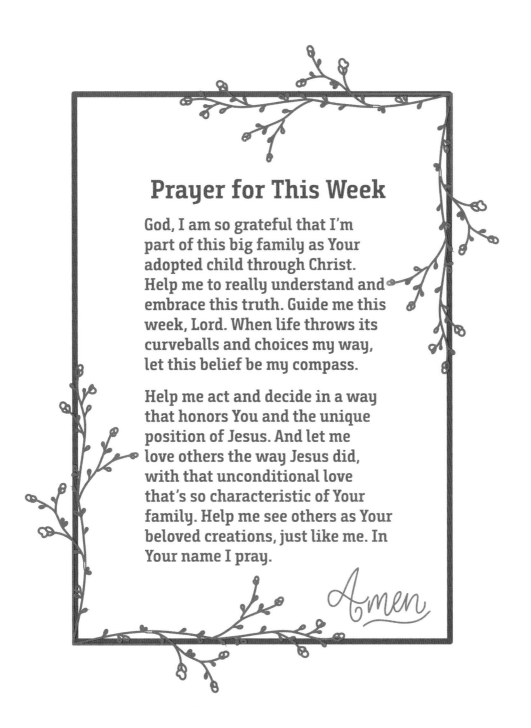

Prayer for This Week

God, I am so grateful that I'm part of this big family as Your adopted child through Christ. Help me to really understand and embrace this truth. Guide me this week, Lord. When life throws its curveballs and choices my way, let this belief be my compass.

Help me act and decide in a way that honors You and the unique position of Jesus. And let me love others the way Jesus did, with that unconditional love that's so characteristic of Your family. Help me see others as Your beloved creations, just like me. In Your name I pray.

Amen

23.

How did Jesus, being the only begotten Son of God, become man?

Jesus, although eternally God and co-equal with the Father and the Holy Spirit, was supernaturally conceived by the power of the Holy Spirit in the womb of the Virgin Mary (Matt. 1:18–23), begotten not created (John 1:14), and was born of her, with a human body and soul, yet without sin (Heb. 7:26).

"Therefore the Lord himself shall give you a sign; Behold, a virgin shall conceive, and bear a son, and shall call his name Immanuel."

Isaiah 7:14

"Now the birth of Jesus Christ was on this wise: When as his mother Mary was espoused to Joseph, before they came together, she was found with child of the Holy Ghost. Then Joseph her husband, being a just man, and not willing to make her a public example, was minded to put her away privily. But while he thought on these things, behold, the angel of the Lord appeared unto him in a dream, saying, Joseph, thou son of David, fear not to take unto thee Mary thy wife: for that which is conceived in her is of the Holy Ghost. And she shall bring forth a son, and thou shalt call his name JESUS: for he shall save his people from their sins. Now all this was done, that it might be fulfilled which was spoken of the Lord by the prophet, saying, Behold, a virgin shall be with child, and shall bring forth a son, and they shall call his name Emmanuel, which being interpreted is, God with us."

Matthew 1:18–23

"And, behold, thou shalt conceive in thy womb, and bring forth a son, and shalt call his name JESUS.... And the angel answered and said unto her, The Holy Ghost shall come upon thee, and the power of the Highest shall overshadow thee: therefore also that holy thing which shall be born of thee shall be called the Son of God."

Luke 1:31, 35

"And the Word was made flesh, and dwelt among us, (and we beheld his glory, the glory as of the only begotten of the Father), full of grace and truth."

John 1:14

"For such an high priest became us, who is holy, harmless, undefiled, separate from sinners, and made higher than the heavens."

Hebrews 7:26

FOUNDATIONAL TRUTH #23
Supernaturally conceived by the Spirit

In Action

Take a few minutes each day, perhaps during your morning routine or before bed, to reflect on the miraculous nature of Jesus' birth. Thank God for sending Jesus into the world in such a unique and significant way. Ponder how this truth impacts your faith and relationship with Him. Feel free to personalize this reflection time to suit your routine and preferences. What does it mean to you that God sent His Son to walk the earth like us?

Definitions

Espoused

This often refers to being betrothed or committed to a spouse in a marriage covenant; also engaged or promised to be married.

Privily

Privately or discreetly.

Immanuel

A name of Hebrew origin, which means "God is with us."

Scripture Checklist

- ■ Isaiah 7:14
- ■ Matthew 1:18–23
- ■ Luke 1:31, 35
- ■ John 1:14
- ■ Hebrews 7:26

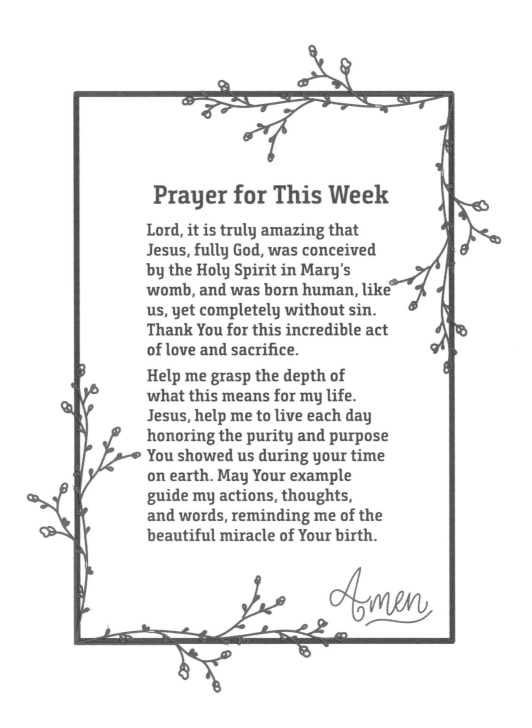

Prayer for This Week

Lord, it is truly amazing that Jesus, fully God, was conceived by the Holy Spirit in Mary's womb, and was born human, like us, yet completely without sin. Thank You for this incredible act of love and sacrifice.

Help me grasp the depth of what this means for my life. Jesus, help me to live each day honoring the purity and purpose You showed us during your time on earth. May Your example guide my actions, thoughts, and words, reminding me of the beautiful miracle of Your birth.

Amen

24. Did Jesus sin during His lifetime?

Jesus was fully human (John 1:14) as we are, but He lived His life on earth without sin (2 Cor. 5:21; Heb. 4:15; 1 Pet. 2:22).

"And he made his grave with the wicked, and with the rich in his death; because he had done no violence, neither was any deceit in his mouth."

Isaiah 53:9

"And the Word was made flesh, and dwelt among us, (and we beheld his glory, the glory as of the only begotten of the Father), full of grace and truth."

John 1:14

"For he hath made him to be sin for us, who knew no sin; that we might be made the righteousness of God in him."

2 Corinthians 5:21

"For we have not an high priest which cannot be touched with the feeling of our infirmities; but was in all points tempted like as we are, yet without sin."

Hebrews 4:15

"For such an high priest became us, who is holy, harmless, undefiled, separate from sinners, and made higher than the heavens."

Hebrews 7:26

"Who did no sin, neither was guile found in his mouth."

1 Peter 2:22

"And ye know that he was manifested to take away our sins; and in him is no sin."

1 John 3:5

In Action

This week, take some time each day to reflect on how Jesus, being fully human, lived a sinless life. Then, consciously strive to emulate His character in your daily choices and interactions. Before acting or speaking, pause and ask yourself, "What would Jesus do or say in this situation?" When faced with conflict or hurt, practice forgiveness just as Jesus did. Ask for wisdom and the ability to resist temptations that might lead you away from a life pleasing to God.

Definitions

Deceit

The act of intentionally misleading or tricking others, often through dishonesty or cunning.

Infirmities

Physical or moral weaknesses, deficiencies, or limitations.

Undefiled

Pure, untainted, free from impurity or corruption, often referring to a state of moral or spiritual purity.

Scripture Checklist

- ☐ Isaiah 53:9
- ☐ John 1:14
- ☐ 2 Corinthians 5:21
- ☐ Hebrews 4:15
- ☐ Hebrews 7:26
- ☐ 1 Peter 2:22
- ☐ 1 John 3:5

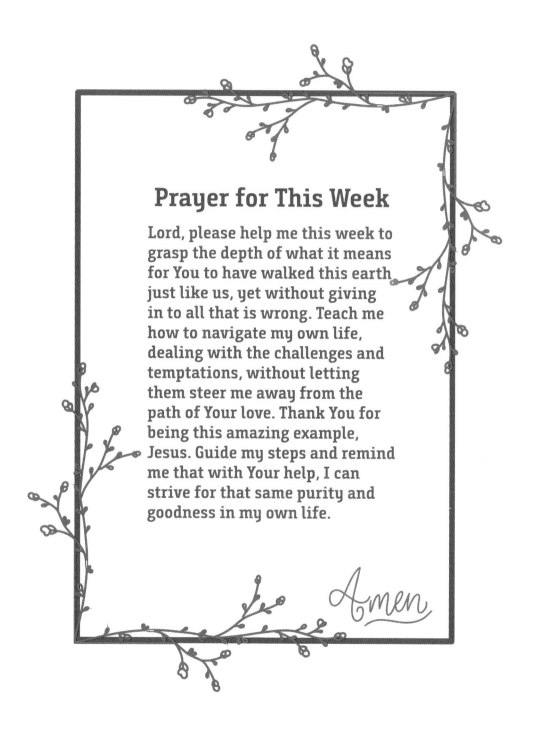

Prayer for This Week

Lord, please help me this week to grasp the depth of what it means for You to have walked this earth just like us, yet without giving in to all that is wrong. Teach me how to navigate my own life, dealing with the challenges and temptations, without letting them steer me away from the path of Your love. Thank You for being this amazing example, Jesus. Guide my steps and remind me that with Your help, I can strive for that same purity and goodness in my own life.

Amen

25. How did Jesus purchase our salvation?

To pay for sin, a sacrifice of blood (Exod. 12:13; Heb. 9:22) must be made from one who was perfect (1 Pet. 1:18–19). Jesus, the Son of God, was the only one to live a sinless life (Heb. 9:12–15) and therefore the only one who could atone for our sin.

"And the blood shall be to you for a token upon the houses where ye are: and when I see the blood, I will pass over you, and the plague shall not be upon you to destroy you, when I smite the land of Egypt."

Exodus 12:13

"For the life of the flesh is in the blood: and I have given it to you upon the altar to make an atonement for your souls: for it is the blood that maketh an atonement for the soul."

Leviticus 17:11

"Neither by the blood of goats and calves, but by his own blood he entered in once into the holy place, having obtained eternal redemption for us. For if the blood of bulls and of goats, and the ashes of an heifer sprinkling the unclean, sanctifieth to the purifying of the flesh: How much more shall the blood of Christ, who through the eternal Spirit offered himself without spot to God, purge your conscience from dead works to serve the living God? And for this cause he is the mediator of the new testament, that by means of death, for the redemption of the transgressions that were under the first testament, they which are called might receive the promise of eternal inheritance."

Hebrews 9:12–15

"And almost all things are by the law purged with blood; and without shedding of blood is no remission."

Hebrews 9:22

"Forasmuch as ye know that ye were not redeemed with corruptible things, as silver and gold, from your vain conversation received by tradition from your fathers; But with the precious blood of Christ, as of a lamb without blemish and without spot."

1 Peter 1:18–19

"But if we walk in the light, as he is in the light, we have fellowship one with another, and the blood of Jesus Christ his Son cleanseth us from all sin."

1 John 1:7

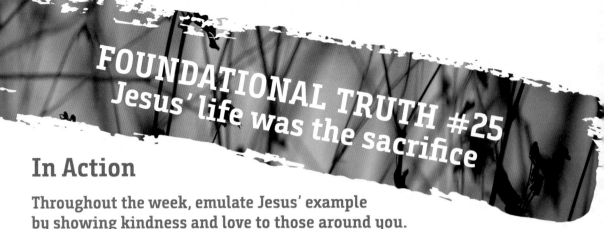

FOUNDATIONAL TRUTH #25
Jesus' life was the sacrifice

In Action

Throughout the week, emulate Jesus' example
by showing kindness and love to those around you.
Whether it's helping someone in need, offering encouragement,
or simply listening and being there for a friend, let your actions reflect
the love and sacrifice Jesus made for us. Remember, living out this belief
involves not only understanding the theological aspect but also embodying
the love and compassion that Jesus demonstrated in His sinless life. It's
about gratitude, sharing the message of hope, and reflecting Jesus' love in
your everyday interactions.

Definitions

Atone

To make amends or reparation for a
wrongdoing; to reconcile or make right a
relationship, particularly in the context of
reconciliation between humans and God.

Purged

The act of cleansing, purifying, or
eliminating impurities, sin, or wrongdoing.

Salvation

Deliverance or rescue from sin, spiritual
death, and the consequences of sin, leading
to eternal life with God.

Scripture Checklist

- ☐ Exodus 12:13
- ☐ Leviticus 17:11
- ☐ Hebrews 9:12–15
- ☐ Hebrews 9:22
- ☐ 1 Peter 1:18–19
- ☐ 1 John 1:7

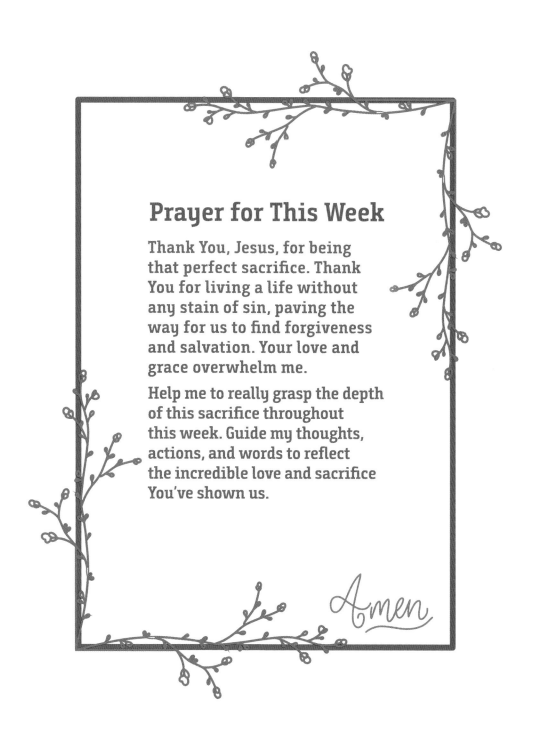

Prayer for This Week

Thank You, Jesus, for being that perfect sacrifice. Thank You for living a life without any stain of sin, paving the way for us to find forgiveness and salvation. Your love and grace overwhelm me.

Help me to really grasp the depth of this sacrifice throughout this week. Guide my thoughts, actions, and words to reflect the incredible love and sacrifice You've shown us.

Amen

26. By what manner did Jesus die?

Jesus died of His own submission (John 10:17–18) to the will of the Father (Isa. 53:10; Acts 2:23), by crucifixion by the Romans (John 19:15–16), after accusations from the elders, scribes, and Sanhedrin (Mark 15:1).

"Yet it pleased the LORD to bruise him; he hath put him to grief: when thou shalt make his soul an offering for sin, he shall see his seed, he shall prolong his days, and the pleasure of the LORD shall prosper in his hand."

Isaiah 53:10

"And straightway in the morning the chief priests held a consultation with the elders and scribes and the whole council, and bound Jesus, and carried him away, and delivered him to Pilate."

Mark 15:1

"Therefore doth my Father love me, because I lay down my life, that I might take it again. No man taketh it from me, but I lay it down of myself. I have power to lay it down, and I have power to take it again. This commandment have I received of my Father."

John 10:17–18

"But they cried out, Away with him, away with him, crucify him. Pilate saith unto them, Shall I crucify your King? The chief priests answered, We have no king but Caesar. Then delivered he him therefore unto them to be crucified. And they took Jesus and led him away."

John 19:15–16

"Him, being delivered by the determinate counsel and foreknowledge of God, ye have taken, and by wicked hands have crucified and slain."

Acts 2:23

"Be it known unto you all, and to all the people of Israel, that by the name of Jesus Christ of Nazareth, whom ye crucified, whom God raised from the dead, even by him doth this man stand here before you whole."

Acts 4:10

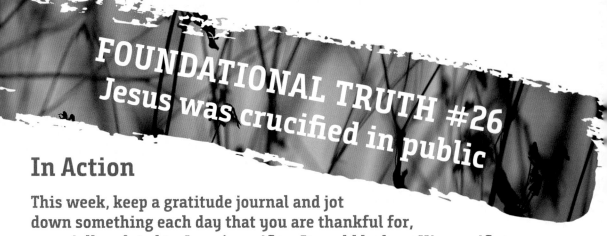

FOUNDATIONAL TRUTH #26
Jesus was crucified in public

In Action

This week, keep a gratitude journal and jot down something each day that you are thankful for, especially related to Jesus' sacrifice. It could be how His sacrifice has impacted your life, the hope it provides, or the love you've experienced through it. Throughout the week, perform small acts of kindness and compassion for others, inspired by Jesus' selfless sacrifice. Whether it's helping someone in need, offering a kind word, or volunteering your time, let your actions reflect the love and sacrifice that Jesus showed us.

Definitions

Anointed

Consecrated, chosen, or set apart for a special purpose, often referring to being spiritually blessed or appointed for a specific service or mission.

Crucified

The act of execution or putting to death by nailing or binding a person to a cross, historically a form of capital punishment.

Foreknowledge

God's perfect knowledge or awareness of all events, actions, and choices, including those of the future, from eternity past.

Scripture Checklist

- [ ] Isaiah 53:10
- [ ] Mark 15:1
- [ ] John 10:17–18
- [ ] John 19:15–16
- [ ] Acts 2:23
- [ ] Acts 4:10

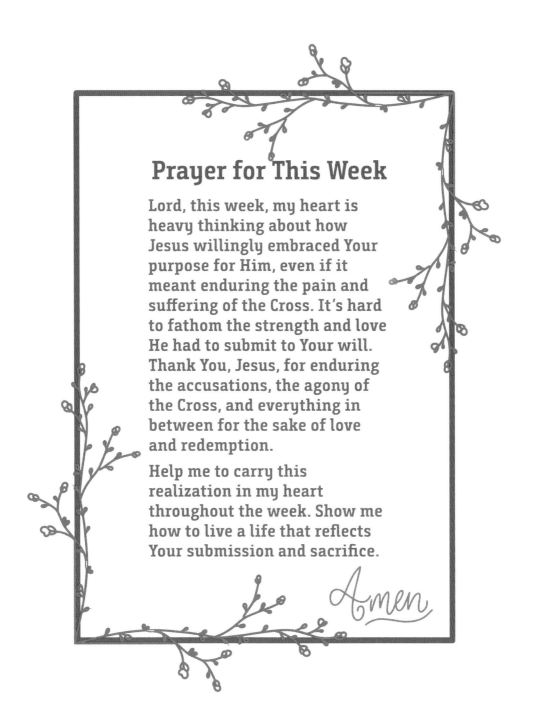

Prayer for This Week

Lord, this week, my heart is heavy thinking about how Jesus willingly embraced Your purpose for Him, even if it meant enduring the pain and suffering of the Cross. It's hard to fathom the strength and love He had to submit to Your will. Thank You, Jesus, for enduring the accusations, the agony of the Cross, and everything in between for the sake of love and redemption.

Help me to carry this realization in my heart throughout the week. Show me how to live a life that reflects Your submission and sacrifice.

Amen

27. How do we know Jesus rose from the dead?

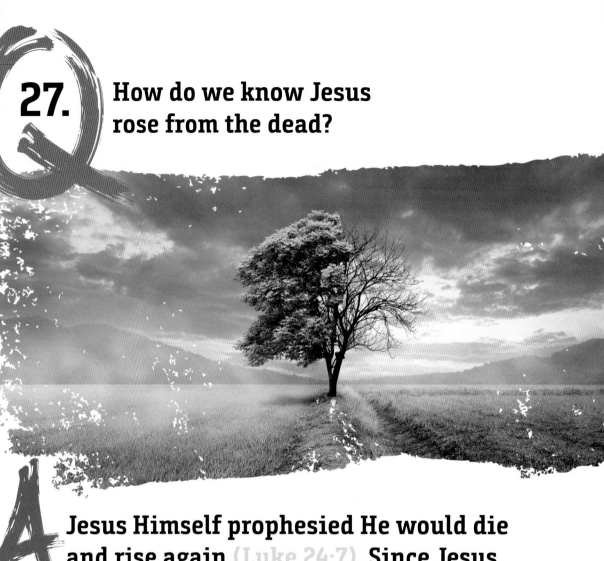

Jesus Himself prophesied He would die and rise again (Luke 24:7). Since Jesus is God and cannot lie, He fulfilled His promise. Multiple witnesses tell us that, after His bodily resurrection from the dead, Jesus appeared to many people, including His disciples (Mark 16:12–13), over five hundred witnesses at one time, and the Apostle Paul (on the road to Damascus).

"Now when Jesus was risen early the first day of the week, he appeared first to Mary Magdalene, out of whom he had cast seven devils. And she went and told them that had been with him, as they mourned and wept. And they, when they had heard that he was alive, and had been seen of her, believed not."

Mark 16:9–11

"After that he appeared in another form unto two of them, as they walked, and went into the country. And they went and told it unto the residue: neither believed they them."

Mark 16:12–13

"Afterward he appeared unto the eleven as they sat at meat, and upbraided them with their unbelief and hardness of heart, because they believed not them which had seen him after he was risen."

Mark 16:14

"Saying, The Son of man must be delivered into the hands of sinful men, and be crucified, and the third day rise again."

Luke 24:7

"And it came to pass, as he sat at meat with them, he took bread, and blessed it, and brake, and gave to them. And their eyes were opened, and they knew him; and he vanished out of their sight. And they said one to another, Did not our heart burn within us, while he talked with us by the way, and while he opened to us the scriptures? And they rose up the same hour, and returned to Jerusalem, and found the eleven gathered together, and them that were with them, Saying, The Lord is risen indeed, and hath appeared to Simon."

Luke 24:30–34

In Action

This week, keep a gratitude journal and jot down something each day that you are thankful for, especially related to Jesus' sacrifice. It could be how His sacrifice has impacted your life, the hope it provides, or the love you've experienced through it. Throughout the week, perform small acts of kindness and compassion for others, inspired by Jesus' selfless sacrifice. Whether it's helping someone in need, offering a kind word, or volunteering your time, let your actions reflect the love and sacrifice that Jesus showed us.

Definitions

Disciples

Individuals who follow and adhere to the teachings, beliefs, or practices of a particular leader, teacher, or philosophy.

Emmaus

A village where two disciples of Jesus were traveling on the day of Jesus' resurrection. They encountered the resurrected Jesus on the road to Emmaus, but they did not recognize him until he broke bread with them, at which point they realized who he was.

Upbraided

To scold, reproach, or criticize someone.

Scripture Checklist

- [ ] Mark 16:9–11
- [ ] Mark 16:12–13
- [ ] Mark 16:14
- [ ] Luke 24:7
- [ ] Luke 24:30–34

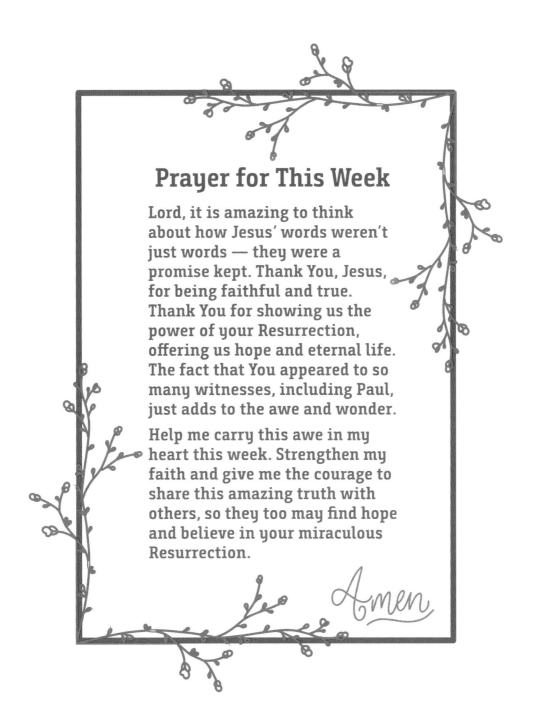

Prayer for This Week

Lord, it is amazing to think about how Jesus' words weren't just words — they were a promise kept. Thank You, Jesus, for being faithful and true. Thank You for showing us the power of your Resurrection, offering us hope and eternal life. The fact that You appeared to so many witnesses, including Paul, just adds to the awe and wonder.

Help me carry this awe in my heart this week. Strengthen my faith and give me the courage to share this amazing truth with others, so they too may find hope and believe in your miraculous Resurrection.

Amen

28. What happened to Jesus after His Resurrection from the dead?

Jesus ascended into heaven where He lives forever, ruling and reigning at the right hand of the Father (Mark 16:19).

"So then after the Lord had spoken unto them, he was received up into heaven, and sat on the right hand of God."

Mark 16:19

"And when he had spoken these things, while they beheld, he was taken up; and a cloud received him out of their sight. And while they looked stedfastly toward heaven as he went up, behold, two men stood by them in white apparel; Which also said, Ye men of Galilee, why stand ye gazing up into heaven? this same Jesus, which is taken up from you into heaven, shall so come in like manner as ye have seen him go into heaven."

Acts 1:9–11

"This Jesus hath God raised up, whereof we all are witnesses. Therefore being by the right hand of God exalted, and having received of the Father the promise of the Holy Ghost, he hath shed forth this, which ye now see and hear."

Acts 2:32–33

"But he, being full of the Holy Ghost, looked up stedfastly into heaven, and saw the glory of God, and Jesus standing on the right hand of God, And said, Behold, I see the heavens opened, and the Son of man standing on the right hand of God."

Acts 7:55–56

"Wherefore God also hath highly exalted him, and given him a name which is above every name: That at the name of Jesus every knee should bow, of things in heaven, and things in earth, and things under the earth; And that every tongue should confess that Jesus Christ is Lord, to the glory of God the Father."

Philippians 2:9–11

"And he came and took the book out of the right hand of him that sat upon the throne."

Revelation 5:7

In Action

Take a few minutes during the day to reflect on the significance of Jesus' ascension. Consider how His position of authority brings hope, comfort, and direction to your life. Express gratitude for His love and sovereignty. Before going to bed, offer a prayer surrendering your concerns and worries to Jesus, acknowledging His reign and trusting in His plans. By consciously acknowledging Jesus' ascension and expressing gratitude for His ongoing role as ruler and guide, you can cultivate a deeper sense of faith and trust in His presence and authority in your daily life.

Definitions

Ascended

To rise or go up, often used in a Christian context to refer to Jesus Christ's ascent into heaven after His Resurrection.

Confess

To openly acknowledge or declare a statement or belief in someone or something.

Exalted

Raised to a high rank, status, or position of honor and praise.

Scripture Checklist

- ☐ Mark 16:19
- ☐ Acts 1:9–11
- ☐ Acts 2:32–33
- ☐ Acts 7:55–56
- ☐ Philippians 2:9–11
- ☐ Revelation 5:7

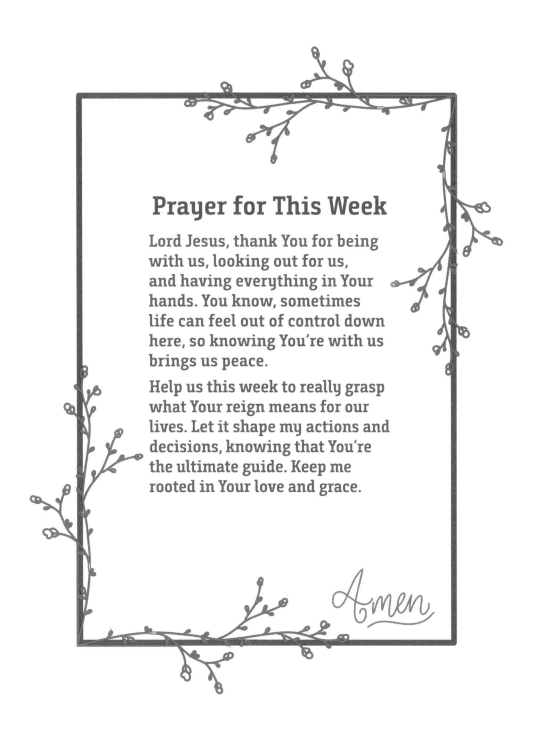

Prayer for This Week

Lord Jesus, thank You for being with us, looking out for us, and having everything in Your hands. You know, sometimes life can feel out of control down here, so knowing You're with us brings us peace.

Help us this week to really grasp what Your reign means for our lives. Let it shape my actions and decisions, knowing that You're the ultimate guide. Keep me rooted in Your love and grace.

Amen

29.

What must we do to be saved?

We must repent of our sins (Acts 2:37–39; 3:19a) and believe on the atoning work of the Lord Jesus Christ alone.

"He that believeth on him is not condemned: but he that believeth not is condemned already, because he hath not believed in the name of the only begotten Son of God."

John 3:18

"He that believeth on the Son hath everlasting life: and he that believeth not the Son shall not see life; but the wrath of God abideth on him."

John 3:36

"Now when they heard this, they were pricked in their heart, and said unto Peter and to the rest of the apostles, Men and brethren, what shall we do? Then Peter said unto them, Repent, and be baptized every one of you in the name of Jesus Christ for the remission of sins, and ye shall receive the gift of the Holy Ghost. For the promise is unto you, and to your children, and to all that are afar off, even as many as the Lord our God shall call."

Acts 2:37–39

"Repent ye therefore, and be converted, that your sins may be blotted out."

Acts 3:19a

"And brought them out, and said, Sirs, what must I do to be saved? And they said, Believe on the Lord Jesus Christ, and thou shalt be saved, and thy house'."

Acts 16:30–31

"But shewed first unto them of Damascus, and at Jerusalem, and throughout all the coasts of Judaea, and then to the Gentiles, that they should repent and turn to God, and do works meet for repentance."

Acts 26:20

FOUNDATIONAL TRUTH #29
We must repent and believe to be saved

In Action

Begin each day by acknowledging your need for repentance and expressing gratitude for Jesus' atoning work. Thank Him for His sacrifice and the opportunity to turn away from sin. Engage in a heartfelt prayer, confessing any known sins and asking for forgiveness. Repent sincerely, seeking to align your thoughts, actions, and desires with God's will. By making daily reflection, prayer, and affirmation a part of your routine, you can consciously cultivate a spirit of repentance and belief, drawing closer to Jesus Christ and embracing His atoning work in your life.

Definitions

Believe

To have faith, trust, and conviction in Jesus Christ as Lord and Savior, accepting His teachings, life, death, and Resurrection as central to one's faith and salvation.

Remission

The act of forgiving or pardoning sins, often used in the context of Christianity to signify the forgiveness and cleansing of sins through faith in Jesus Christ.

Repent

Feeling genuine remorse and sorrow for one's sins or wrongdoings, leading to a change of heart, mind, and behavior, often accompanied by a turning toward God.

Scripture Checklist

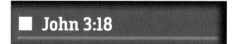
- [ ] John 3:18

- [ ] John 3:36

- [ ] Acts 2:37–39

- [ ] Acts 3:19a

- [ ] Acts 16:30–31

- [ ] Acts 26:20

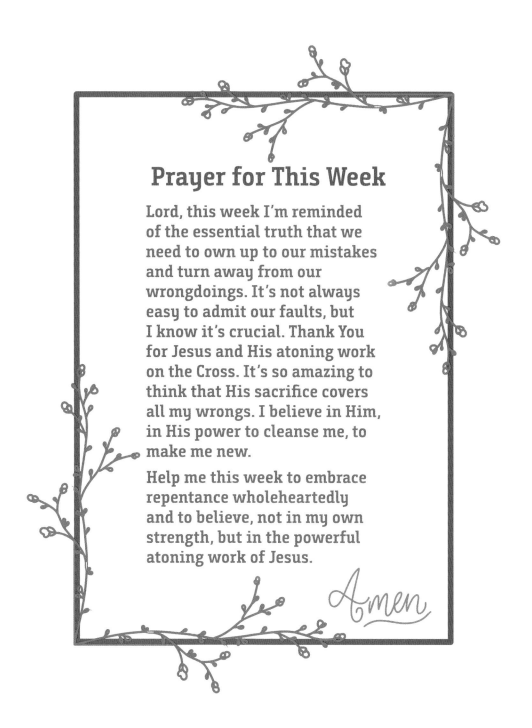

Prayer for This Week

Lord, this week I'm reminded of the essential truth that we need to own up to our mistakes and turn away from our wrongdoings. It's not always easy to admit our faults, but I know it's crucial. Thank You for Jesus and His atoning work on the Cross. It's so amazing to think that His sacrifice covers all my wrongs. I believe in Him, in His power to cleanse me, to make me new.

Help me this week to embrace repentance wholeheartedly and to believe, not in my own strength, but in the powerful atoning work of Jesus.

Amen

30. What is Justification?

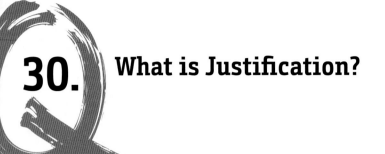

Justification is an act of God's free grace, wherein He pardons all our sins, and accepts us as righteous in His sight, only for the righteousness of Christ imputed to us and received by faith alone (Rom. 3:24).

"Be it known unto you therefore, men and brethren, that through this man is preached unto you the forgiveness of sins: And by him all that believe are justified from all things, from which ye could not be justified by the law of Moses."

Acts 13:38–39

"Therefore by the deeds of the law there shall no flesh be justified in his sight: for by the law is the knowledge of sin."

Romans 3:20

"Being justified freely by his grace through the redemption that is in Christ Jesus."

Romans 3:24

"Moreover whom he did predestinate, them he also called: and whom he called, them he also justified: and whom he justified, them he also glorified."

Romans 8:30

"Knowing that a man is not justified by the works of the law, but by the faith of Jesus Christ, even we have believed in Jesus Christ, that we might be justified by the faith of Christ, and not by the works of the law: for by the works of the law shall no flesh be justified."

Galatians 2:16

FOUNDATIONAL TRUTH #30
God makes us fully righteous

In Action

Start your day by expressing gratitude to God for the gift of justification. Thank Him for pardoning your sins and accepting you as righteous through Christ's righteousness, which you receive by faith alone. Consider how being justified by God completely changes how He sees you and what that means for you as you go through your day.

Definitions

Glorified

To be exalted, honored, or praised in the highest degree, often referring to the state of being elevated or exalted to a divine or heavenly status.

Justification

Being declared or made righteous in the sight of God through faith in Jesus Christ.

Righteousness

This is often associated with a state of being in right relationship with God, obtained through faith in Jesus Christ, leading to a life that aligns with God's principles and teachings.

Scripture Checklist

- ☐ Acts 13:38–39
- ☐ Romans 3:20
- ☐ Romans 3:24
- ☐ Romans 8:30
- ☐ Galatians 2:16

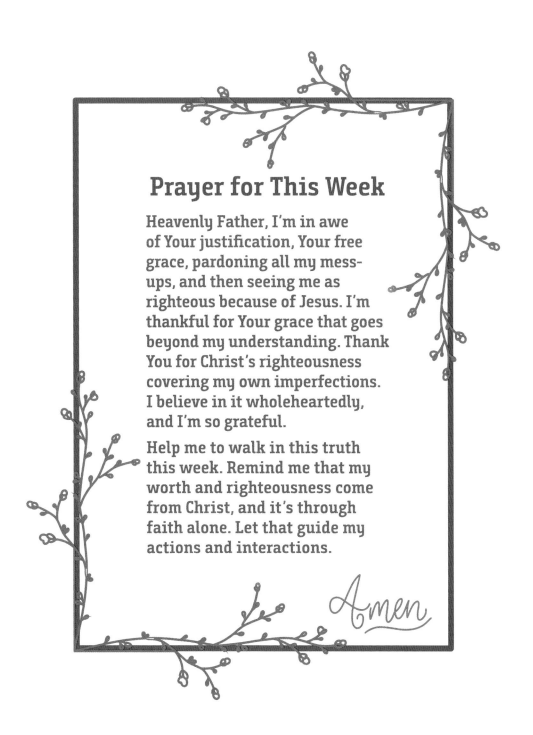

Prayer for This Week

Heavenly Father, I'm in awe of Your justification, Your free grace, pardoning all my mess-ups, and then seeing me as righteous because of Jesus. I'm thankful for Your grace that goes beyond my understanding. Thank You for Christ's righteousness covering my own imperfections. I believe in it wholeheartedly, and I'm so grateful.

Help me to walk in this truth this week. Remind me that my worth and righteousness come from Christ, and it's through faith alone. Let that guide my actions and interactions.

Amen

31.

What does it mean to be born again?

To be born again means we have been regenerated (made new) by the power of the Holy Spirit (2 Cor. 5:17).

"A new heart also will I give you, and a new spirit will I put within you: and I will take away the stony heart out of your flesh, and I will give you an heart of flesh."

Ezekiel 36:26

"Jesus answered and said unto him, Verily, verily, I say unto thee, Except a man be born again, he cannot see the kingdom of God. Nicodemus saith unto him, How can a man be born when he is old? can he enter the second time into his mother's womb, and be born? Jesus answered, Verily, verily, I say unto thee, Except a man be born of water and of the Spirit, he cannot enter into the kingdom of God. That which is born of the flesh is flesh; and that which is born of the Spirit is spirit. Marvel not that I said unto thee, Ye must be born again."

John 3:3–7

"Therefore if any man be in Christ, he is a new creature: old things are passed away; behold, all things are become new."

2 Corinthians 5:17

"Not by works of righteousness which we have done, but according to his mercy he saved us, by the washing of regeneration, and renewing of the Holy Ghost."

Titus 3:5

FOUNDATIONAL TRUTH #31
Being born again is being made new

In Action

Take a moment each day to reflect on how your life has changed since you decided to follow Jesus. Thank God for the transformation and growth you've experienced. Look for opportunities to help and encourage others. It could be as simple as lending a listening ear, offering a helping hand, or sharing a word of encouragement. Show the love and kindness that God has shown you.

Definitions

Regenerated

Being made spiritually new or born again through faith in Jesus Christ, experiencing a transformation of the heart and spirit by the work of the Holy Spirit.

Renewing

The ongoing process of spiritual growth and transformation in a believer's life, involving the renewal of the mind, character, and behavior to align with God's will and purposes.

Washing

Symbolizing the spiritual cleansing and purifying of a person's soul through faith in Jesus Christ, often associated with baptism and the forgiveness of sins.

Scripture Checklist

- ☐ Ezekiel 36:26
- ☐ John 3:3–7
- ☐ 2 Corinthians 5:17
- ☐ Titus 3:5

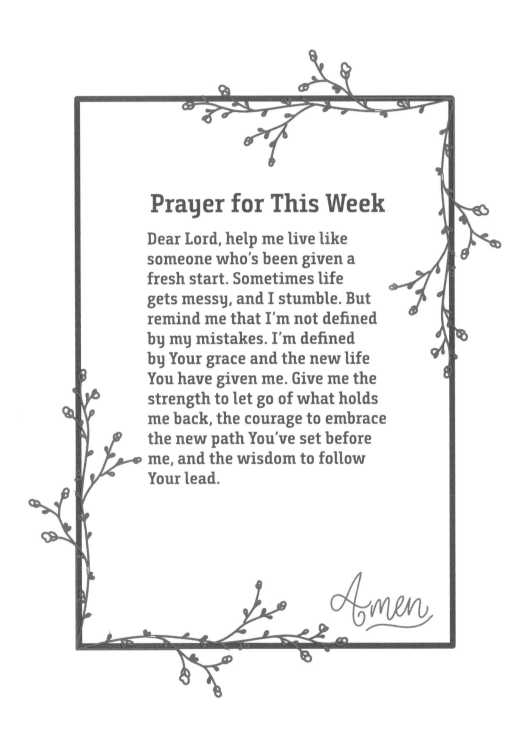

Prayer for This Week

Dear Lord, help me live like someone who's been given a fresh start. Sometimes life gets messy, and I stumble. But remind me that I'm not defined by my mistakes. I'm defined by Your grace and the new life You have given me. Give me the strength to let go of what holds me back, the courage to embrace the new path You've set before me, and the wisdom to follow Your lead.

Amen

32. Can we be saved by our own good works?

No, we are saved by grace, through faith, in Christ alone (Eph. 2:8-9).

"But we are all as an unclean thing, and all our righteousnesses are as filthy rags; and we all do fade as a leaf; and our iniquities, like the wind, have taken us away."

Isaiah 64:6

"But we believe that through the grace of the Lord Jesus Christ we shall be saved, even as they."

Acts 15:11

"So then it is not of him that willeth, nor of him that runneth, but of God that sheweth mercy."

Romans 9:16

"And if by grace, then is it no more of works: otherwise grace is no more grace. But if it be of works, then is it no more grace: otherwise work is no more work."

Romans 11:6

"Even when we were dead in sins, hath quickened us together with Christ (by grace ye are saved)."

Ephesians 2:5

"For by grace are ye saved through faith; and that not of yourselves: it is the gift of God: Not of works, lest any man should boast."

Ephesians 2:8–9

"And you, being dead in your sins and the uncircumcision of your flesh, hath he quickened together with him, having forgiven you all trespasses."

Colossians 2:13

In Action

Set a goal to show unconditional love and kindness to at least one person each day. It could be a friend, family member, coworker, or even a stranger. Just show them some genuine care and support, with no expectations in return. It's like a daily dose of grace and kindness, just as we believe we've received grace through faith in Christ. Remember, actions speak louder than words. So, let your love and kindness be the testimony of the grace you've received.

Definitions

Grace

God's unmerited favor and love toward humanity, especially in the context of salvation and forgiveness of sins.

Iniquities

Immoral or sinful actions, behaviors, or thoughts that go against God.

Works

Things we do as a result of our salvation to demonstrate thankfulness to God and love to others. They do not earn God's favor or salvation.

Scripture Checklist

- ☐ Isaiah 64:6
- ☐ Acts 15:11
- ☐ Romans 9:16
- ☐ Romans 11:6
- ☐ Ephesians 2:5
- ☐ Ephesians 2:8–9
- ☐ Colossians 2:13

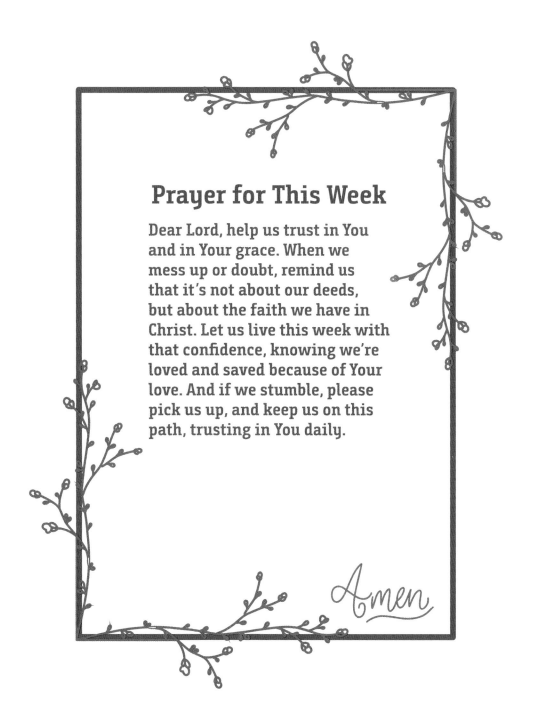

Prayer for This Week

Dear Lord, help us trust in You and in Your grace. When we mess up or doubt, remind us that it's not about our deeds, but about the faith we have in Christ. Let us live this week with that confidence, knowing we're loved and saved because of Your love. And if we stumble, please pick us up, and keep us on this path, trusting in You daily.

Amen

33. Is there another way to be saved besides trusting in the sacrifice of Jesus Christ as the only atonement for our sin?

There is no other means of salvation, and no other savior, but Christ alone (John 14:6).

"Verily, verily, I say unto you, He that entereth not by the door into the sheepfold, but climbeth up some other way, the same is a thief and a robber. But he that entereth in by the door is the shepherd of the sheep."

John 10:1–2

"Then said Jesus unto them again, Verily, verily, I say unto you, I am the door of the sheep. All that ever came before me are thieves and robbers: but the sheep did not hear them. I am the door: by me if any man enter in, he shall be saved, and shall go in and out, and find pasture. The thief cometh not, but for to steal, and to kill, and to destroy: I am come that they might have life, and that they might have it more abundantly."

John 10:7–10

"Jesus said to her, I am the resurrection, and the life: he that believeth in me, though he were dead, yet shall he live."

John 11:25

"Jesus saith unto him, I am the way, the truth, and the life: no man cometh unto the Father, but by me."

John 14:6

"Neither is there salvation in any other: for there is none other name under heaven given among men, whereby we must be saved."

Acts 4:12

"For there is one God, and one mediator between God and men, the man Christ Jesus."

1 Timothy 2:5

In Action

Every day, take a few moments to reflect — maybe in the morning or evening. Reflect on your faith and the belief that Christ is the only Savior. Consider how this impacts your life and the way you interact with others. Thank God for His salvation and ask for guidance to live according to His teachings. Then let that heart of thanks fill your whole week.

Definitions

Atonement

Jesus made us right before God through His death on the cross.

Mediator

A go-between or intercessor who bridges the gap between God and humanity.

Sheepfold

Signifies a place of safety, protection, and guidance under the care and leadership of a shepherd tending to his flock.

Scripture Checklist

- [ ] John 10:1–2
- [ ] John 10:7–10
- [ ] John 11:25
- [ ] John 14:6
- [ ] Acts 4:12
- [ ] 1 Timothy 2:5

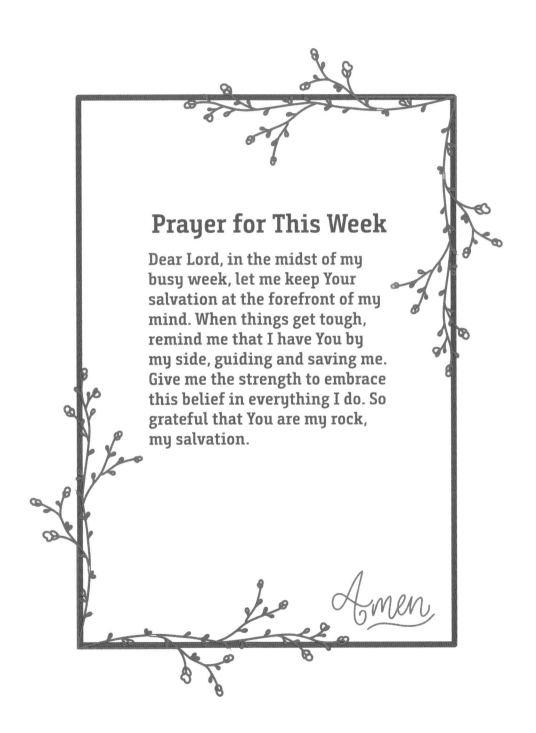

Prayer for This Week

Dear Lord, in the midst of my busy week, let me keep Your salvation at the forefront of my mind. When things get tough, remind me that I have You by my side, guiding and saving me. Give me the strength to embrace this belief in everything I do. So grateful that You are my rock, my salvation.

Amen

34. What is true saving faith?

Saving faith is more than mental agreement to a list of doctrines (James 2:14–22). True belief (saving faith) results in surrendering completely to the Lordship of Jesus Christ (Luke 9:23–24; Rom. 10:9). Obeying Jesus' teachings is the evidence of being truly saved.

"And he said to them all, If any man will come after me, let him deny himself, and take up his cross daily, and follow me. For whosoever will save his life shall lose it: but whosoever will lose his life for my sake, the same shall save it."

Luke 9:23–24

"That if thou shalt confess with thy mouth the Lord Jesus, and shalt believe in thine heart that God hath raised him from the dead, thou shalt be saved."

Romans 10:9

"What doth it profit, my brethren, though a man say he hath faith, and have not works? can faith save him? If a brother or sister be naked, and destitute of daily food, and one of you say unto them, Depart in peace, be ye warmed and filled; notwithstanding ye give them not those things which are needful to the body; what doth it profit? Even so faith, if it hath not works, is dead, being alone. Yea, a man may say, Thou hast faith, and I have works: shew me thy faith without thy works, and I will shew thee my faith by my works. Thou believest that there is one God; thou doest well: the devils also believe, and tremble. But wilt thou know, O vain man, that faith without works is dead? Was not Abraham our father justified by works, when he had offered Isaac his son upon the altar? Seest thou how faith wrought with his works, and by works was faith made perfect?"

James 2:14–22

In Action

Every day, take a moment to reflect on your faith and actions. Ask yourself: Am I merely acknowledging Jesus' teachings, or am I actively surrendering to His lordship and obeying what He taught? Periodically pause and reflect on the decisions and actions you're making through the day. Remember, it's about actively living out your faith, not just agreeing with doctrines. Each day is an opportunity to strengthen your belief by putting it into action.

Definitions

Deny

To let go of one's own desires, ambitions, and self-centeredness in order to follow and prioritize God's will.

Doctrine

A set of beliefs or teachings that are fundamental to faith; the core beliefs of Christianity.

Justified

To be declared righteous by God based on faith in Jesus Christ and His atoning sacrifice.

Scripture Checklist

- [ ] Luke 9:23–24
- [ ] Romans 10:9
- [ ] James 2:14–22

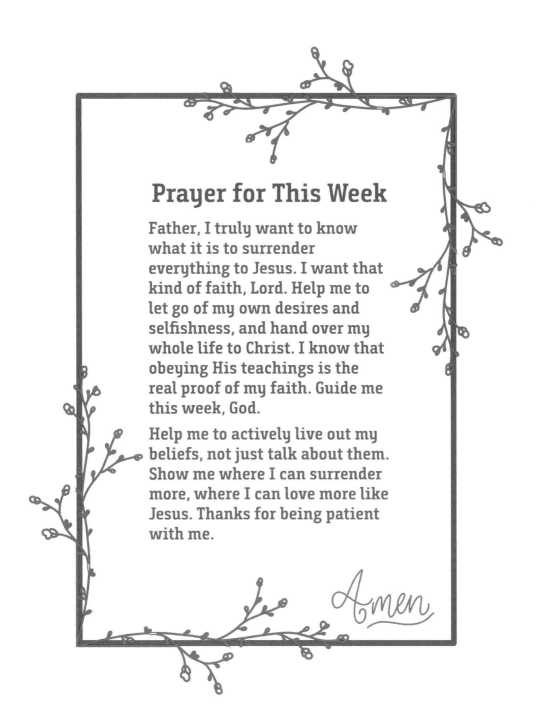

Prayer for This Week

Father, I truly want to know what it is to surrender everything to Jesus. I want that kind of faith, Lord. Help me to let go of my own desires and selfishness, and hand over my whole life to Christ. I know that obeying His teachings is the real proof of my faith. Guide me this week, God.

Help me to actively live out my beliefs, not just talk about them. Show me where I can surrender more, where I can love more like Jesus. Thanks for being patient with me.

Amen

35. Why must Christians obey God?

Christians do not obey God in order to become saved, but rather as an evidence or fruit of truly being saved (1 John 2:3–4). We obey God to honor Him.

"Not every one that saith unto me, Lord, Lord, shall enter into the kingdom of heaven; but he that doeth the will of my Father which is in heaven."

Matthew 7:21

"But he said, 'Yea rather, blessed are they that hear the word of God, and keep it."

Luke 11:28

"If ye love me, keep my commandments."

John 14:15

"He that hath my commandments, and keepeth them, he it is that loveth me: and he that loveth me shall be loved of my Father, and I will love him, and will manifest myself to him."

John 14:21

"Then Peter and the other apostles answered and said, We ought to obey God rather than men."

Acts 5:29

"Even when we were dead in sins, hath quickened us together with Christ (by grace ye are saved)."

Ephesians 2:5

"And hereby we do know that we know him, if we keep his commandments. He that saith, I know him, and keepeth not his commandments, is a liar, and the truth is not in him."

1 John 2:3–4

In Action

Reflect on your actions each night this week.
Before going to bed, take a few minutes to reflect on your day.
Consider your actions, decisions, and interactions. Ask yourself if they
reflected your desire to honor God. If you realize areas where you fell short,
acknowledge them and ask for forgiveness and strength to do better. By
incorporating personal reflection into your daily routine, you'll actively
honor God through your actions and grow in your faith. Remember, it's all
about living in a way that shows your love and appreciation for God.

Definitions

Blessed

Favored; experiencing the goodness and
grace of God in one's life.

Fruit

Refers to the qualities or attributes that
Christians should develop in their lives as
evidence of the Holy Spirit's presence.

Manifest

To show or reveal something clearly or
make it evident, often used in the context
of revealing spiritual gifts, qualities, or
divine presence.

Scripture Checklist

- [ ] Matthew 7:21
- [ ] Luke 11:28
- [ ] John 14:15
- [ ] John 14:21
- [ ] Acts 5:29
- [ ] Ephesians 2:5
- [ ] 1 John 2:3-4

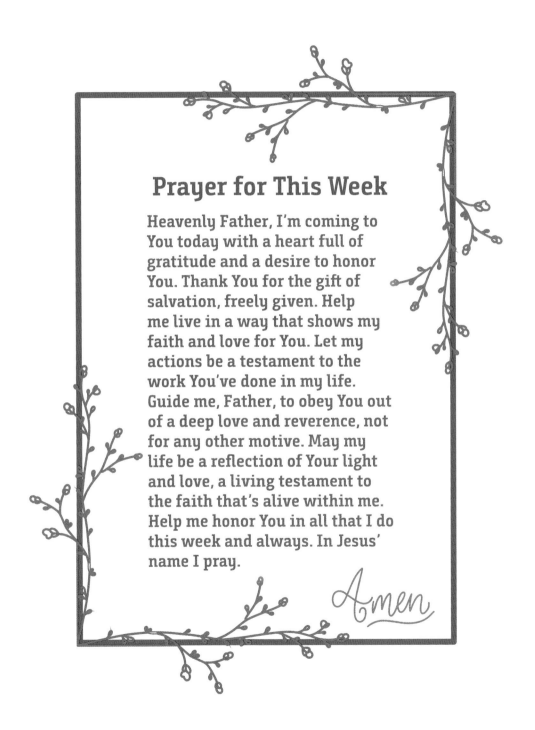

Prayer for This Week

Heavenly Father, I'm coming to You today with a heart full of gratitude and a desire to honor You. Thank You for the gift of salvation, freely given. Help me live in a way that shows my faith and love for You. Let my actions be a testament to the work You've done in my life. Guide me, Father, to obey You out of a deep love and reverence, not for any other motive. May my life be a reflection of Your light and love, a living testament to the faith that's alive within me. Help me honor You in all that I do this week and always. In Jesus' name I pray.

Amen

36. Q What is the greatest commandment?

A To love God first, and then to love your neighbor (Luke 10:27).

"Thou shalt love the Lord thy God with all thy heart, and with all thy soul, and with all thy strength, and with all thy mind; and thy neighbour as thyself." — **Luke 10:27**

"For God so loved the world, that he gave his only begotten Son, that whosoever believeth in him should not perish, but have everlasting life." — **John 3:16**

"But God commendeth his love toward us, in that, while we were yet sinners, Christ died for us." — **Romans 5:8**

"Love worketh no ill to his neighbour: therefore love is the fulfilling of the law." — **Romans 13:10**

"My little children, let us not love in word, neither in tongue; but in deed and in truth." — **1 John 3:18**

"Beloved, let us love one another: for love is of God; and every one that loveth is born of God, and knoweth God." — **1 John 4:7**

"In this was manifested the love of God toward us, because that God sent his only begotten Son into the world, that we might live through him. Herein is love, not that we loved God, but that he loved us, and sent his Son to be the propitiation for our sins." — **1 John 4:9-10**

In Action

Throughout the week, intentionally perform small acts of kindness for others. It could be as simple as holding the door open, giving a genuine compliment, or helping someone in need. These acts reflect God's love in action. Also, reach out to your neighbors or members of your community. Invite them for a meal or just have a friendly conversation. Show interest in their lives and let them know you care. Building these connections is a great way to demonstrate love. Remember, it's the small, genuine actions that make a big difference.

Definitions

Love

A deep and selfless affection, care, and goodwill toward others, reflecting God's love for humanity as expressed through Jesus Christ.

Neighbor

Not only someone who lives nearby but anyone around us, embodying the idea of showing kindness, compassion, and love to all people, regardless of proximity.

Heart

Often used to symbolize the innermost center of a person's being—the seat of their thoughts, emotions, intentions, and spiritual life. It's seen as the source of a person's character, beliefs, and relationship with God.

Scripture Checklist

- ☐ Luke 10:27
- ☐ John 3:16
- ☐ Romans 5:8
- ☐ Romans 13:10
- ☐ 1 John 3:18
- ☐ 1 John 4:7
- ☐ 1 John 4:9-10

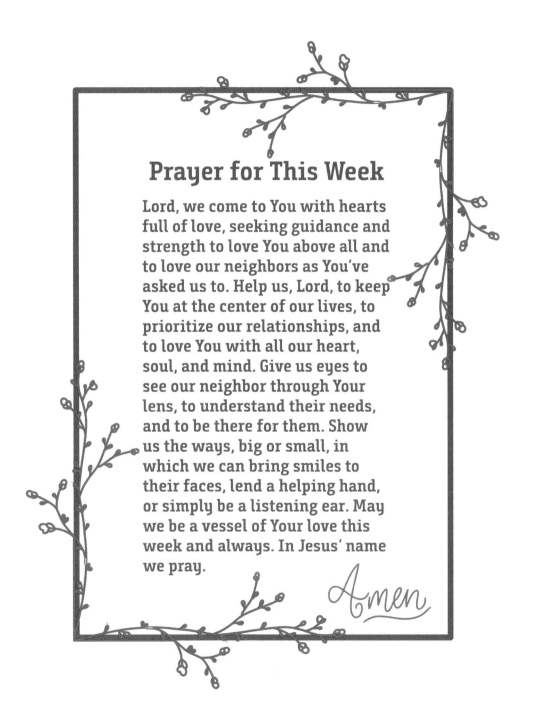

Prayer for This Week

Lord, we come to You with hearts full of love, seeking guidance and strength to love You above all and to love our neighbors as You've asked us to. Help us, Lord, to keep You at the center of our lives, to prioritize our relationships, and to love You with all our heart, soul, and mind. Give us eyes to see our neighbor through Your lens, to understand their needs, and to be there for them. Show us the ways, big or small, in which we can bring smiles to their faces, lend a helping hand, or simply be a listening ear. May we be a vessel of Your love this week and always. In Jesus' name we pray.

Amen

37. What is my duty to my neighbor?

God commands me to love my neighbor as myself (Luke 10:27; 1 Pet. 1:22), tell the truth about him (Exod. 20:16), refuse to covet anything he has (Deut. 5:21), esteem him as better than myself (Phil. 2:3), serve him (Gal. 5:13), and do him no harm (Rom. 13:10).

"Thou shalt not bear false witness against thy neighbour." **Exodus 20:16**

"Ye shall not steal, neither deal falsely, neither lie one to another." **Leviticus 19:11**

"Neither shalt thou desire thy neighbour's wife, neither shalt thou covet thy neighbour's house, his field, or his manservant, or his maidservant, his ox, or his ass, or any thing that is thy neighbour's." **Deuteronomy 5:21**

"Thou shalt love ... thy neighbour as thyself." **Luke 10:27**

"Love worketh no ill to his neighbour: therefore love is the fulfilling of the law." **Romans 13:10**

"For, brethren, ye have been called unto liberty; only use not liberty for an occasion to the flesh, but by love serve one another." **Galatians 5:13**

"Let nothing be done through strife or vainglory; but in lowliness of mind let each esteem other better than themselves." **Philippians 2:3**

"Seeing ye have purified your souls in obeying the truth through the Spirit unto unfeigned love of the brethren, see that ye love one another with a pure heart fervently." **1 Peter 1:22**

In Action

Take some time to really connect with a neighbor.
Maybe it's the guy next door, or the lady down the hall. Invite them
for coffee or a chat on the porch. Show them kindness and genuine care.
Above all, be real. Speak the truth, but do it with love and kindness. Lift
each other up and treat everyone like they
matter, because they do. Let's make this
week about genuine love and respect for
those around You.

Definitions

Covet

To strongly desire or long for something
that belongs to someone else, often leading
to envy or greed.

Liberty

The freedom and rights granted by God to
individuals.

Vainglory

Excessive pride, boasting, or a desire for
recognition and admiration from others
for one's own achievements or qualities. It
is seen as a negative quality that distracts
from a focus on humility and serving God.

Scripture Checklist

- [ ] Exodus 20:16
- [ ] Leviticus 19:11
- [ ] Deuteronomy 5:21
- [ ] Luke 10:27
- [ ] Romans 13:10
- [ ] Galatians 5:13
- [ ] Philippians 2:3
- [ ] 1 Peter 1:22

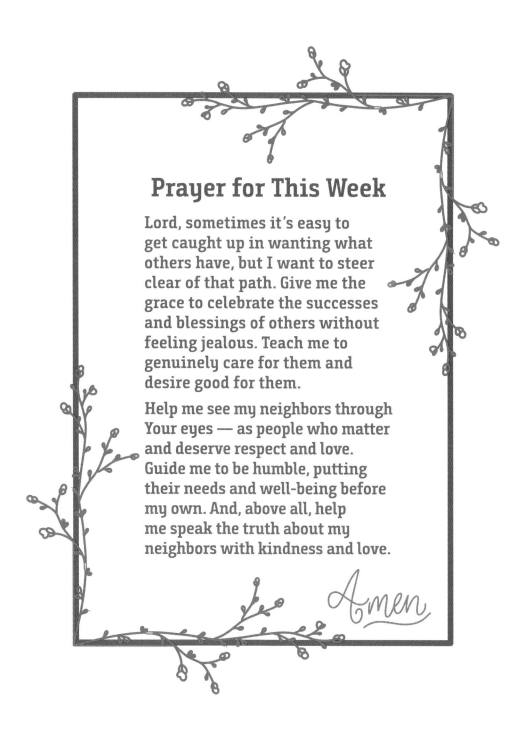

Prayer for This Week

Lord, sometimes it's easy to get caught up in wanting what others have, but I want to steer clear of that path. Give me the grace to celebrate the successes and blessings of others without feeling jealous. Teach me to genuinely care for them and desire good for them.

Help me see my neighbors through Your eyes — as people who matter and deserve respect and love. Guide me to be humble, putting their needs and well-being before my own. And, above all, help me speak the truth about my neighbors with kindness and love.

Amen

38. What is Sanctification?

Sanctification is the process where God cleanses us through the power of the Holy Spirit and sets us apart to Himself for His service (2 Thess. 2:13).

"I beseech you therefore, brethren, by the mercies of God, that ye present your bodies a living sacrifice, holy, acceptable unto God, which is your reasonable service."

Romans 12:1

"But of him are ye in Christ Jesus, who of God is made unto us wisdom, and righteousness, and sanctification, and redemption."

1 Corinthians 1:30

"And such were some of you: but ye are washed, but ye are sanctified, but ye are justified in the name of the Lord Jesus, and by the Spirit of our God."

1 Corinthians 6:11

And the very God of peace sanctify you wholly; and I pray God your whole spirit and soul and body be preserved blameless unto the coming of our Lord Jesus Christ. Faithful is he that calleth you, who also will do it."

1 Thessalonians 5:23–24

"But we are bound to give thanks alway to God for you, brethren beloved of the Lord, because God hath from the beginning chosen you to salvation through sanctification of the Spirit and belief of the truth."

2 Thessalonians 2:13

"If a man therefore purge himself from these, he shall be a vessel unto honour, sanctified, and meet for the master's use, and prepared unto every good work."

2 Timothy 2:21

FOUNDATIONAL TRUTH #38
Sanctification is God's cleansing through the Spirit

In Action

Take a moment each day this week to pray and invite the Holy Spirit to work in your life. Ask for guidance, strength, and wisdom to live in a way that honors God. Identify one area in your life where you struggle or could grow spiritually (e.g., patience, kindness, self-control). Ask the Spirit to show you changes you can make this week. Find a Bible verse or passage that resonates with you about sanctification. Write it down or set it as a reminder on your phone and reflect on it daily.

Definitions

Redemption

The act of being saved or rescued from sin and its consequences through the atoning sacrifice of Jesus Christ.

Sanctification

The process of being set apart, purified, and made holy through the work of the Holy Spirit in a believer's life, leading to a life of righteousness and obedience to God.

Vessel

A person who allows themselves to be used by God for honorable and righteous purposes.

Scripture Checklist

- [ ] Romans 12:1
- [ ] 1 Corinthians 1:30
- [ ] 1 Corinthians 6:11
- [ ] 1 Thessalonians 5:23–24
- [ ] 2 Thessalonians 2:13
- [ ] 2 Timothy 2:21

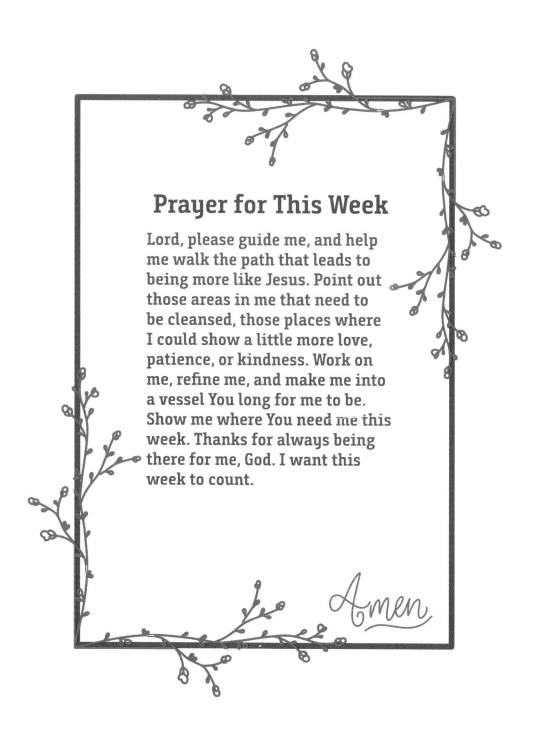

Prayer for This Week

Lord, please guide me, and help me walk the path that leads to being more like Jesus. Point out those areas in me that need to be cleansed, those places where I could show a little more love, patience, or kindness. Work on me, refine me, and make me into a vessel You long for me to be. Show me where You need me this week. Thanks for always being there for me, God. I want this week to count.

Amen

39. When will Jesus return?

No one knows the day or hour of Jesus' return, except the Father (Matt. 24:36-37).

"But of that day and hour knoweth no man, no, not the angels of heaven, but my Father only. But as the days of Noah were, so shall also the coming of the Son of man be…. Watch therefore: for ye know not what hour your Lord doth come. But know this, that if the goodman of the house had known in what watch the thief would come, he would have watched, and would not have suffered his house to be broken up. Therefore be ye also ready: for in such an hour as ye think not the Son of man cometh."

Matthew 24:36–37, 42–44)

"But of that day and that hour knoweth no man, no, not the angels which are in heaven, neither the Son, but the Father. Take ye heed, watch and pray: for ye know not when the time is. For the Son of man is as a man taking a far journey, who left his house, and gave authority to his servants, and to every man his work, and commanded the porter to watch. Watch ye therefore: for ye know not when the master of the house cometh, at even, or at midnight, or at the cockcrowing, or in the morning: Lest coming suddenly he find you sleeping. And what I say unto you I say unto all, Watch."

Mark 13:32–37

"Let your loins be girded about, and your lights burning; And ye yourselves like unto men that wait for their lord, when he will return from the wedding; that when he cometh and knocketh, they may open unto him immediately. Blessed are those servants, whom the lord when he cometh shall find watching: verily I say unto you, that he shall gird himself, and make them to sit down to meat, and will come forth and serve them. And if he shall come in the second watch, or come in the third watch, and find them so, blessed are those servants."

Luke 12:35–38

FOUNDATIONAL TRUTH #39
Only the Father knows when Jesus will return

In Action

Consider this week how your life should be lived each day in view of the Lord's return. Be kind, honest, and treat others with love and respect. Live a life that aligns with your beliefs. Let go of grudges and forgive those who have wronged you. It's important to keep your heart clear and ready for Jesus, whenever He comes back. If the opportunity arises, share your faith and the hope you have in Jesus. Let others know that no matter when He comes back, you're living in a way that reflects your belief in His return.

Definitions

Girded

Typically refers to being spiritually prepared or strengthened for a task or challenge.

Son of man

A phrase used in the Bible, often used by Jesus to refer to Himself, signifying both His humanity and divine mission as the Messiah, connecting with the prophetic language used in the Old Testament.

Watch

Staying alert, vigilant, and spiritually aware of the signs of the times, particularly in anticipation of Jesus' return.

Scripture Checklist

- Matthew 24:36–37, 42–44)
- Mark 13:32–37
- Luke 12:35–38

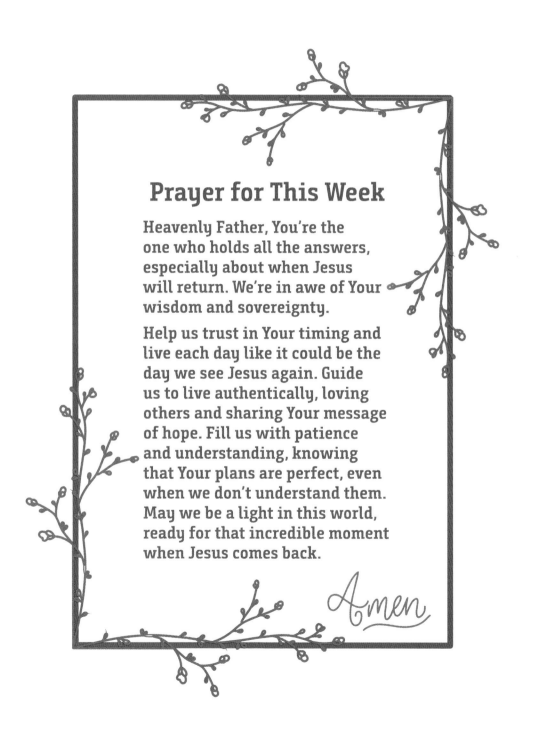

Prayer for This Week

Heavenly Father, You're the one who holds all the answers, especially about when Jesus will return. We're in awe of Your wisdom and sovereignty.

Help us trust in Your timing and live each day like it could be the day we see Jesus again. Guide us to live authentically, loving others and sharing Your message of hope. Fill us with patience and understanding, knowing that Your plans are perfect, even when we don't understand them. May we be a light in this world, ready for that incredible moment when Jesus comes back.

Amen

40. In what manner will Jesus return?

Jesus will return in the clouds of heaven in the glory of His father with His angels (Matt. 16:27).

"For the Son of man shall come in the glory of his Father with his angels; and then he shall reward every man according to his works."

Matthew 16:27

"Jesus saith unto him, Thou hast said: nevertheless I say unto you, Hereafter shall ye see the Son of man sitting on the right hand of power, and coming in the clouds of heaven."

Matthew 26:64

"Which also said, Ye men of Galilee, why stand ye gazing up into heaven? this same Jesus, which is taken up from you into heaven, shall so come in like manner as ye have seen him go into heaven."

Acts 1:11

"For the Lord himself shall descend from heaven with a shout, with the voice of the archangel, and with the trump of God: and the dead in Christ will rise first: Then we which are alive and remain shall be caught up together with them in the clouds, to meet the Lord in the air: and so shall we ever be with the Lord."

1 Thessalonians 4:16–17

"And I saw heaven opened, and behold a white horse; and he that sat upon him was called Faithful and True, and in righteousness he doth judge and make war. His eyes were as a flame of fire, and on his head were many crowns; and he had a name written, that no man knew, but he himself. And he was clothed with a vesture dipped in blood: and his name is called The Word of God. And the armies which were in heaven followed him upon white horses, clothed in fine linen, white and clean. And out of his mouth goeth a sharp sword, that with it he should smite the nations: and he shall rule them with a rod of iron: and he treadeth the winepress of the fierceness and wrath of Almighty God. And he hath on his vesture and on his thigh a name written, KING OF KINGS, AND LORD OF LORDS."

Revelation 19:11-16

In Action

This week, send a message or make a call to someone who could use some encouragement. Be the messenger of hope. Approach challenges with a positive attitude. Show that Jesus' return brings hope and joy. Take time to pray for those you know and even those you don't. Pray for their well-being, peace, and understanding of Jesus' love.

Definitions

Archangel

A high-ranking angel, often associated with important messages or tasks, and believed to have significant roles in God's divine plan, seen as powerful beings in the spiritual realm.

Heaven

The eternal abode of God, a place of perfect and eternal bliss, joy, and peace, often described as a place free from sin, suffering, and all earthly troubles, where believers are in the presence of God and experience eternal happiness.

Return

Refers to the anticipated event of Jesus Christ's second coming to Earth, as prophesied in the Bible; the belief that Jesus will return to judge the living and the dead and to rule over God's eternal kingdom.

Scripture Checklist

- [ ] Matthew 16:27
- [ ] Matthew 26:64
- [ ] Acts 1:11
- [ ] 1 Thessalonians 4:16–17
- [ ] Revelation 19:11-16

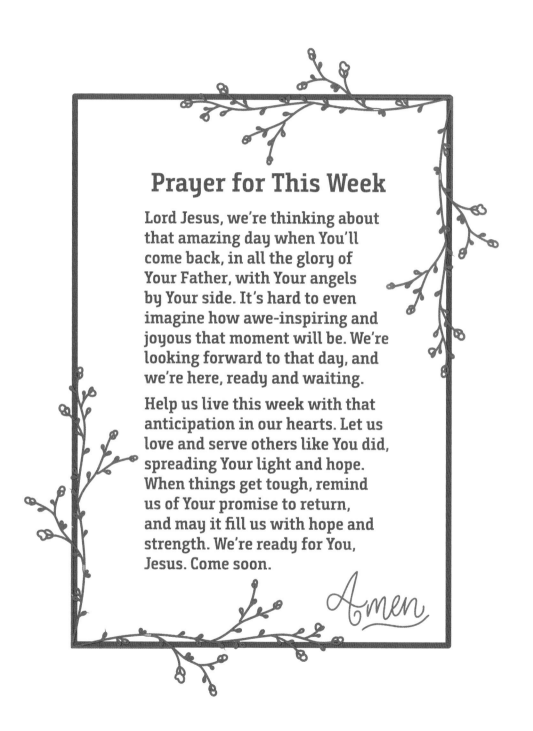

Prayer for This Week

Lord Jesus, we're thinking about that amazing day when You'll come back, in all the glory of Your Father, with Your angels by Your side. It's hard to even imagine how awe-inspiring and joyous that moment will be. We're looking forward to that day, and we're here, ready and waiting.

Help us live this week with that anticipation in our hearts. Let us love and serve others like You did, spreading Your light and hope. When things get tough, remind us of Your promise to return, and may it fill us with hope and strength. We're ready for You, Jesus. Come soon.

Amen

41. What is the Resurrection of the dead?

When Jesus returns, all those who have died believing in Christ will rise again to eternal life, and the unrighteous to judgment and eternal punishment (1 Thess. 4:13-18).

"And this is the will of him that sent me, that every one which seeth the Son, and believeth on him, may have everlasting life: and I will raise him up at the last day."

John 6:40

"Jesus said unto her, I am the resurrection, and the life: he that believeth in me, though he were dead, yet shall he live: And whosoever liveth and believeth in me shall never die. Believest thou this?"

John 11:25–26

"But I would not have you to be ignorant, brethren, concerning them which are asleep, that ye sorrow not, even as others which have no hope. For if we believe that Jesus died and rose again, even so them also which sleep in Jesus will God bring with him. For this we say unto you by the word of the Lord, that we which are alive and remain unto the coming of the Lord shall not prevent them which are asleep. For the Lord himself shall descend from heaven with a shout, with the voice of the archangel, and with the trump of God: and the dead in Christ shall rise first: Then we which are alive and remain shall be caught up together with them in the clouds, to meet the Lord in the air: and so shall we ever be with the Lord. Wherefore comfort one another with these words."

1 Thessalonians 4:13–18

FOUNDATIONAL TRUTH #41
The Resurrection is when all rise to life or punishment

In Action

Take some time this week to reaffirm your faith in Christ and strive to align your actions with the values and principles He taught. Additionally, consider sharing this hope of resurrection and eternal life with someone, encouraging them to also embrace faith in Christ for a brighter future. Remember, small steps of faithfulness can have a big impact.

Definitions

Asleep

A state of physical death or cessation of life in the body, often described as "asleep" in the Bible, reflecting the belief in eventual awakening through resurrection.

Punishment

Those who reject God's salvation, live in a state of sin, and if they do not repent will face everlasting separation from God.

Resurrection

The rising of the dead to life, particularly the central event of Jesus Christ's rising from the dead, signifying victory over sin and death and offering hope of eternal life.

Scripture Checklist

- [ ] John 6:40
- [ ] John 11:25–26
- [ ] 1 Thessalonians 4:13–18

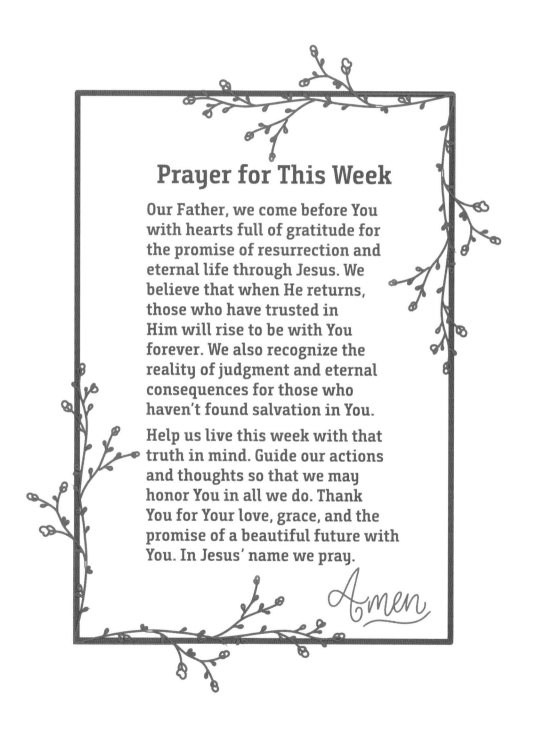

Prayer for This Week

Our Father, we come before You with hearts full of gratitude for the promise of resurrection and eternal life through Jesus. We believe that when He returns, those who have trusted in Him will rise to be with You forever. We also recognize the reality of judgment and eternal consequences for those who haven't found salvation in You.

Help us live this week with that truth in mind. Guide our actions and thoughts so that we may honor You in all we do. Thank You for Your love, grace, and the promise of a beautiful future with You. In Jesus' name we pray.

Amen

42. Whom does the Holy Spirit fill?

The Holy Spirit fills (Acts 8:15–17), baptizes (Matt. 3:11; Acts 1:5; 11:16), and regenerates (Titus 3:5) believers in Jesus.

"I indeed baptize you with water unto repentance, but he that cometh after me is mightier than I, whose shoes I am not worthy to bear: he shall baptize you with the Holy Ghost, and with fire."

Matthew 3:11

"But this spake he of the Spirit, which they that believe on him should receive: for the Holy Ghost was not yet given; because that Jesus was not yet glorified."

John 7:39

"But when the Comforter is come, whom I will send unto you from the Father, even the Spirit of truth, which proceedeth from the Father, he shall testify of me."

John 15:26

"For John truly baptized with water; but ye shall be baptized with the Holy Ghost not many days hence."

Acts 1:5

"And we are his witnesses of these things; and so is also the Holy Ghost, whom God hath given to them that obey him."

Acts 5:32

"Who, when they were come down, prayed for them, that they might receive the Holy Ghost: (For as yet he was fallen upon none of them: only they were baptized in the name of the Lord Jesus.) Then laid they their hands on them, and they received the Holy Ghost."

Acts 8:15–17

"Then remembered I the word of the Lord, how that he said, John indeed baptized with water; but ye shall be baptized with the Holy Ghost."

Acts 11:16

"Not by works of righteousness which we have done, but according to his mercy he saved us, by the washing of regeneration, and renewing of the Holy Ghost."

Titus 3:5

In Action

To really embrace the Holy Spirit's awesome power during the week, take a moment in the evening to reflect on your day. Thank the Holy Spirit for the moments you felt filled, renewed, or guided. Also, acknowledge any areas where you could use more of that divine touch and ask for guidance for the next day. Let that divine empowerment infuse your days and make a difference in the lives of those around you.

Definitions

Baptizes

The spiritual act of the empowering of the Holy Spirit, often associated with conversion into the Christian faith.

Fills

The experience of being infused or saturated with the presence, power, and guidance of the Holy Spirit, bringing spiritual empowerment, joy, and transformation in a person's life.

Regenerates

The spiritual renewal or transformation of a person's heart and life through the work of the Holy Spirit, resulting in a new spiritual birth and a changed, righteous nature.

Scripture Checklist

- ☐ Matthew 3:11
- ☐ John 7:39
- ☐ John 15:26
- ☐ Acts 1:5
- ☐ Acts 5:32
- ☐ Acts 8:15–17
- ☐ Acts 11:16
- ☐ Titus 3:5

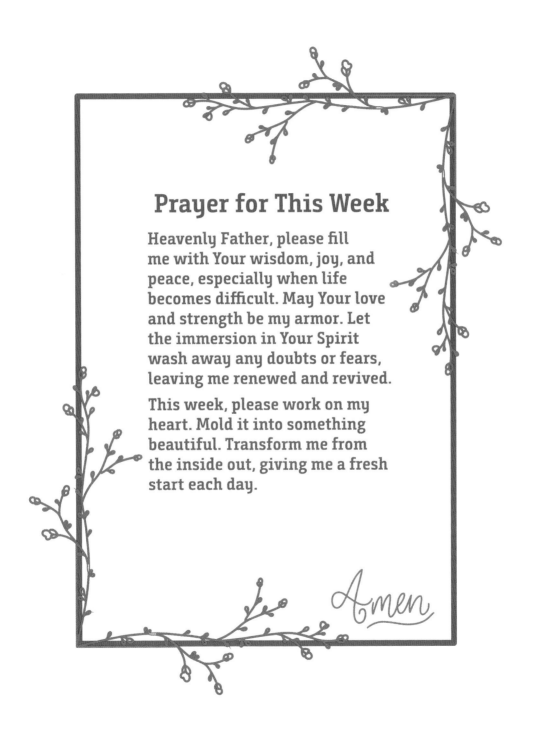

Prayer for This Week

Heavenly Father, please fill me with Your wisdom, joy, and peace, especially when life becomes difficult. May Your love and strength be my armor. Let the immersion in Your Spirit wash away any doubts or fears, leaving me renewed and revived.

This week, please work on my heart. Mold it into something beautiful. Transform me from the inside out, giving me a fresh start each day.

Amen

43. What is the work of the Holy Spirit?

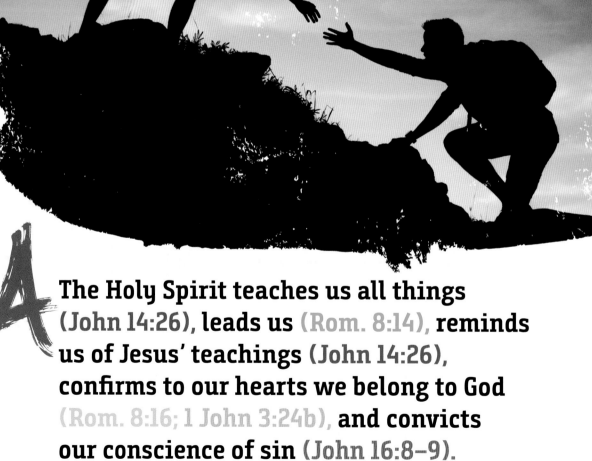

The Holy Spirit teaches us all things (John 14:26), leads us (Rom. 8:14), reminds us of Jesus' teachings (John 14:26), confirms to our hearts we belong to God (Rom. 8:16; 1 John 3:24b), and convicts our conscience of sin (John 16:8–9).

"But the Comforter, which is the Holy Ghost, whom the Father will send in My name, he shall teach you all things, and bring all things to your remembrance, whatsoever I have said unto you."

John 14:26

"And when he is come, he will reprove the world of sin, and of righteousness, and of judgment: Of sin, because they believe not on me."

John 16:8–9

"For as many as are led by the Spirit of God, they are the sons of God."

Romans 8:14

"The Spirit itself beareth witness with our spirit, that we are the children of God."

Romans 8:16

"But if ye be led of the Spirit, ye are not under the law."

Galatians 5:18

"And hereby we know that he abideth in us, by the Spirit which he hath given us."

1 John 3:24b

In Action

Start your day with a cup of coffee (or your favorite beverage) and spend some time reading from the Bible. Let the words soak in and ask the Holy Spirit to guide your understanding. Set a reminder on your phone or jot a note to yourself about a specific teaching of Jesus. Let that reminder pop up during the day, prompting you to reflect on how you can apply that teaching in your life. Remember, it's all about staying connected and being open to the Spirit's guidance in the midst of your everyday routines.

Definitions

Abideth

An older form of the verb "abide," meaning to remain, endure, or persist.

Comforter

Refers to the Holy Spirit, who provides solace, guidance, and support to believers.

Convicts

Typically refers to the action of the Holy Spirit convicting or bringing awareness of sin or wrongdoing in a person's life, leading to repentance and a desire for a changed life.

Scripture Checklist

- [ ] John 14:26
- [ ] John 16:8–9
- [ ] Romans 8:14
- [ ] Romans 8:16
- [ ] Galatians 5:18
- [ ] 1 John 3:24b

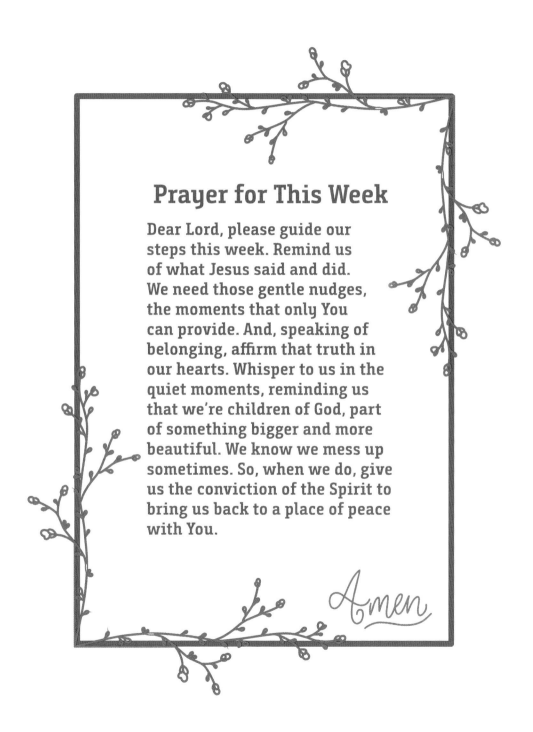

Prayer for This Week

Dear Lord, please guide our steps this week. Remind us of what Jesus said and did. We need those gentle nudges, the moments that only You can provide. And, speaking of belonging, affirm that truth in our hearts. Whisper to us in the quiet moments, reminding us that we're children of God, part of something bigger and more beautiful. We know we mess up sometimes. So, when we do, give us the conviction of the Spirit to bring us back to a place of peace with You.

Amen

44. What is the fruit of the Spirit?

The fruit of the Spirit describes God's attributes that He imparts to those who belong to Him (Gal. 5:22-23).

"I am the vine, ye are the branches: He that abideth in me, and I in him, the same bringeth forth much fruit: for without me ye can do nothing."

John 15:5

"The fruit of the Spirit is love, joy, peace, longsuffering, gentleness, goodness, faith, meekness, temperance."

Galatians 5:22–23

"With all lowliness and meekness, with longsuffering, forbearing one another in love; Endeavouring to keep the unity of the Spirit in the bond of peace."

Ephesians 4:2–3

"And beside this, giving all diligence, add to your faith virtue; and to virtue knowledge; And to knowledge temperance; and to temperance patience; and to patience godliness; And to godliness brotherly kindness; and to brotherly kindness charity. For if these things be in you, and abound, they make you that ye shall neither be barren nor unfruitful in the knowledge of our Lord Jesus Christ."

2 Peter 1:5–8

In Action

Grab some sticky notes and write down each fruit of the Spirit from your biblical translation. Stick them where you'll see them — on your mirror, fridge, or computer. Let these little notes nudge you to embody these qualities throughout the day. When you have your lunchtime, ponder the fruit of the Spirit. Think about how you can apply a specific attribute in your interactions for the rest of the day. Challenge yourself to pick one aspect of the fruit of the Spirit each day and consciously live it out.

Definitions

Diligence

Putting consistent effort and hard work into something, often motivated by a sense of duty, faithfulness, or a desire to honor God. It's about doing your best and persevering with determination.

Meekness

Involves strength under control, where a person remains humble, gentle, and patient even in challenging situations. It's about having a submissive and teachable spirit, yet being strong in character.

Temperance

Exercising self-control and moderation in all aspects of life, such as desires, actions, and choices.

Scripture Checklist

- [ ] John 15:5
- [ ] Galatians 5:22–23
- [ ] Ephesians 4:2–3
- [ ] 2 Peter 1:5–8

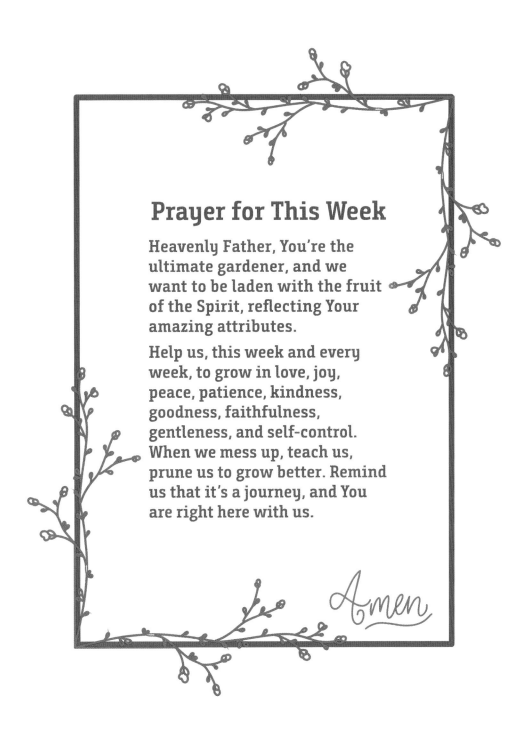

Prayer for This Week

Heavenly Father, You're the ultimate gardener, and we want to be laden with the fruit of the Spirit, reflecting Your amazing attributes.

Help us, this week and every week, to grow in love, joy, peace, patience, kindness, goodness, faithfulness, gentleness, and self-control. When we mess up, teach us, prune us to grow better. Remind us that it's a journey, and You are right here with us.

Amen

45. What is the Church?

The universal church is made up of all true followers of Jesus Christ around the world, since the day of Pentecost. The local church is made up of born-again, baptized believers who live in submission to God and communion and fellowship with one another (Col. 1:18).

"Take heed therefore unto yourselves, and to all the flock, over the which the Holy Ghost hath made you overseers, to feed the church of God, which he hath purchased with his own blood."

Acts 20:28

"For as we have many members in one body, and all members have not the same office: So we, being many, are one body in Christ, and every one members one of another."

Romans 12:4–5

"And God hath set some in the church, first apostles, secondarily prophets, thirdly teachers, after that miracles, then gifts of healings, helps, governments, diversities of tongues."

1 Corinthians 12:28

"Now therefore ye are no more strangers and foreigners, but fellow citizens with the saints, and of the household of God; And are built upon the foundation of the apostles and prophets, Jesus Christ himself being the chief corner stone; In whom all the building fitly framed together groweth unto an holy temple in the Lord: In whom ye also are builded together for an habitation of God through the Spirit."

Ephesians 2:19–22

"And he is the head of the body, the church: who is the beginning, the firstborn from the dead; that in all things he might have the preeminence."

Colossians 1:18

"And let us consider one another to provoke unto love and to good works: Not forsaking the assembling of ourselves together, as the manner of some is; but exhorting one another: and so much the more, as ye see the day approaching."

Hebrews 10:24–25

FOUNDATIONAL TRUTH #45
The church is all followers of Christ

In Action

This week, connect with a fellow follower of Christ from a different part of the world. It could be a simple message or a video call. Swap stories and celebrate the worldwide family we're part of. Set aside some quiet time to pray for the unity of God's church. Ask for God's blessings on all believers worldwide, that we may stand strong in our faith and love for one another.

Definitions

Overseers

Often referred to as bishops or elders, these individuals are appointed to provide spiritual leadership, guidance, and pastoral care.

Pentecost

The significant event described in the Book of Acts. It marks the descent of the Holy Spirit upon the Apostles and other followers of Jesus Christ, 50 days after Jesus' Resurrection.

Preeminence

Denotes the supreme or highest position, authority, or importance of Jesus Christ. It emphasizes the belief that Jesus holds a unique and superior rank above all creation and is the central figure in Christian faith and doctrine.

Scripture Checklist

- [ ] Acts 20:28
- [ ] Romans 12:4–5
- [ ] 1 Corinthians 12:28
- [ ] Ephesians 2:19–22
- [ ] Colossians 1:18
- [ ] Hebrews 10:24–25

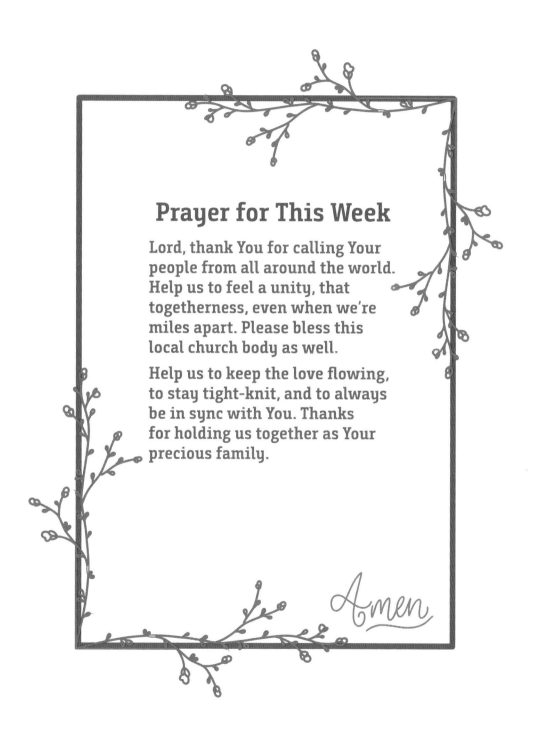

Prayer for This Week

Lord, thank You for calling Your people from all around the world. Help us to feel a unity, that togetherness, even when we're miles apart. Please bless this local church body as well.

Help us to keep the love flowing, to stay tight-knit, and to always be in sync with You. Thanks for holding us together as Your precious family.

Amen

46. What is Baptism?

Baptism with water represents the death of our sinful self and resurrection into newness of life (Rom. 6:3–4).

"Go ye therefore, and teach all nations, baptizing them in the name of the Father, and of the Son, and of the Holy Ghost."

Matthew 28:19

"And he said unto them, Unto what then were ye baptized? And they said, Unto John's baptism. Then said Paul, John verily baptized with the baptism of repentance, saying unto the people, that they should believe on him which should come after him, that is, on Christ Jesus. When they heard this, they were baptized in the name of the Lord Jesus."

Acts 19:3–5

"Know ye not, that so many of us as were baptized into Jesus Christ were baptized into his death? Therefore we are buried with him by baptism into death: that like as Christ was raised up from the dead by the glory of the Father, even so we also should walk in newness of life."

Romans 6:3–4

"For as many of you as have been baptized into Christ have put on Christ."

Galatians 3:27

"Buried with him in baptism, wherein also ye are risen with him through the faith of the operation of God, who hath raised him from the dead."

Colossians 2:12

"The like figure whereunto even baptism doth also now save us (not the putting away of the filth of the flesh, but the answer of a good conscience toward God,) by the resurrection of Jesus Christ."

1 Peter 3:21

FOUNDATIONAL TRUTH #46
Baptism represents our death to life

In Action

Take a moment each day to reflect on your life before your decision to follow Jesus. Remember, the water in baptism represents washing away the sin of the old life. Read Bible passages about baptism and what it signifies. Allow the words to soak into your heart and mind, reinforcing the beautiful transformation that baptism represents. Romans 6:3–4 is a great place to start!

Definitions

Baptism

A Christian sacrament or ordinance involving the immersion or sprinkling of water on a person as a symbol of purification, dedication, and initiation into the community of believers. It's an outward expression of an inward commitment to follow Jesus Christ.

Buried

Often used to symbolize the believer's identification with the death, burial, and Resurrection of Jesus Christ.

Filth

Refers to impurities, sinful desires, or morally corrupt actions associated with the physical and worldly aspects of human existence.

Scripture Checklist

- [ ] Matthew 28:19
- [ ] Acts 19:3–5
- [ ] Romans 6:3–4
- [ ] Galatians 3:27
- [ ] Colossians 2:12
- [ ] 1 Peter 3:21

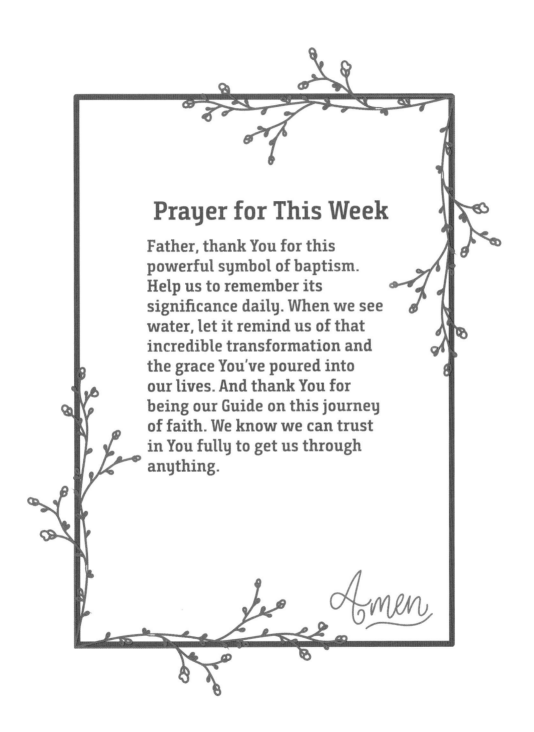

Prayer for This Week

Father, thank You for this powerful symbol of baptism. Help us to remember its significance daily. When we see water, let it remind us of that incredible transformation and the grace You've poured into our lives. And thank You for being our Guide on this journey of faith. We know we can trust in You fully to get us through anything.

Amen

47. What is the Lord's Supper (Communion)?

Communion is eating bread and drinking wine (or grape juice) as a remembrance of the Lord's body being beaten, and His blood being shed, during His death on the Cross (Luke 22:14–20).

"And as they were eating, Jesus took bread, and blessed it, and brake it, and gave it to the disciples, and said, Take, eat; this is my body. And he took the cup, and gave thanks, and gave it to them, saying, Drink ye all of it; For this is my blood of the new testament, which is shed for many for the remission of sins."

Matthew 26:26–28

"And when the hour was come, he sat down, and the twelve apostles with him. And he said unto them, With desire I have desired to eat this passover with you before I suffer: For I say unto you, I will not any more eat thereof, until it be fulfilled in the kingdom of God. And he took the cup, and gave thanks, and said, Take this, and divide it among yourselves: For I say unto you, I will not drink of the fruit of the vine, until the kingdom of God shall come. And he took bread, and gave thanks, and brake it, and gave unto them, saying, This is my body which is given for you: this do in remembrance of me. Likewise also the cup after supper, saying, This cup is the new testament in my blood, which is shed for you."

Luke 22:14-20

"And they continued steadfastly in the apostles' doctrine and fellowship, and in breaking of bread, and in prayers."

Acts 2:42

"The cup of blessing which we bless, is it not the communion of the blood of Christ? The bread which we break, is it not the communion of the body of Christ?"

1 Corinthians 10:16

FOUNDATIONAL TRUTH #47
Through communion we remember the sacrifice of Jesus

In Action

Take time this week to reflect on Jesus' sacrifice. Think about what Jesus went through. Let the weight of it sink in. Remember that Jesus' body was broken for you. Remember Jesus' blood was shed for your redemption and forgiveness. Thank God for His incredible sacrifice and the grace that came from it. Think about how you can live out this love and sacrifice in your week ahead. How can you extend grace and kindness to others?

Definitions

Communion

Also known as the Lord's Supper or the Eucharist, this is a sacrament or ordinance where believers partake of bread and wine (or grape juice) symbolizing the body and blood of Jesus Christ.

Remembrance

Recalling or reflecting upon significant events or teachings, especially related to Jesus Christ, His sacrifice, and the foundational beliefs of the Christian faith.

Remission

The forgiveness or removal of sins, often through repentance and acceptance of Jesus Christ as Savior. It signifies the cleansing of one's soul from the burden of sin and the restoration of a right relationship with God.

Scripture Checklist

- [ ] Matthew 26:26–28
- [ ] Luke 22:14-20
- [ ] Acts 2:42
- [ ] 1 Corinthians 10:16

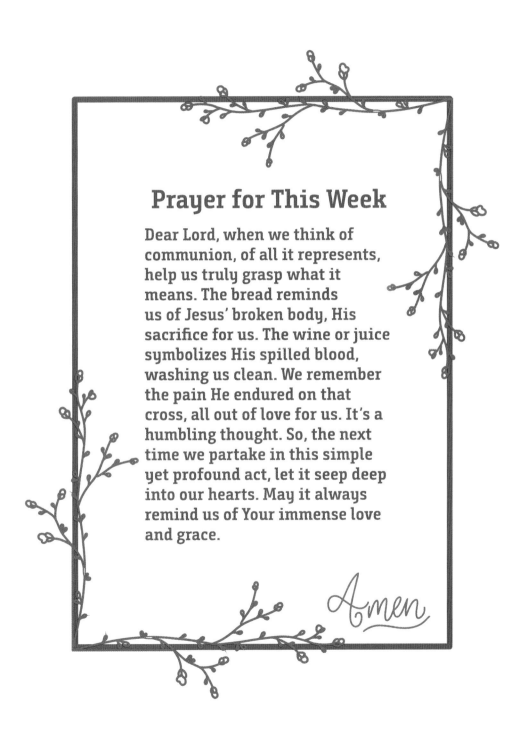

Prayer for This Week

Dear Lord, when we think of communion, of all it represents, help us truly grasp what it means. The bread reminds us of Jesus' broken body, His sacrifice for us. The wine or juice symbolizes His spilled blood, washing us clean. We remember the pain He endured on that cross, all out of love for us. It's a humbling thought. So, the next time we partake in this simple yet profound act, let it seep deep into our hearts. May it always remind us of Your immense love and grace.

Amen

48. What does it mean to worship God?

Worship is giving all we are in response to who God is and what He has done (Rom. 12:1). Worship is more than merely singing. Worship is doing everything we do for the glory of God (1 Cor. 10:31). Worship in Spirit is living according to the character and nature of God (Gal 5:22–23); worship in truth (John 4:23–24) is living according to God's Word that is true and sanctifies us.

"O worship the LORD in the beauty of holiness: fear before him, all the earth."

Psalm 96:9

"But the hour cometh, and now is, when the true worshippers shall worship the Father in spirit and in truth: for the Father seeketh such to worship him. God is a Spirit: and they that worship him must worship him in spirit and in truth."

John 4:23–24

"I beseech you therefore, brethren, by the mercies of God, that ye present your bodies a living sacrifice, holy, acceptable unto God, which is your reasonable service."

Romans 12:1

"Whether therefore ye eat, or drink, or whatsoever ye do, do all to the glory of God."

1 Corinthians 10:31

"But the fruit of the Spirit is love, joy, peace, longsuffering, gentleness, goodness, faith, meekness, temperance: against such there is no law."

Galatians 5:22-23

"Let the word of Christ dwell in you richly in all wisdom; teaching and admonishing one another in psalms and hymns and spiritual songs, singing with grace in your hearts to the Lord. And whatsoever ye do in word or deed, do all in the name of the Lord Jesus, giving thanks to God and the Father by him."

Colossians 3:16-17

In Action

In everything you do this week — whether it's holding the door open for someone, smiling at a stranger, or helping a friend — do it with the mindset of giving glory to God. Let your actions reflect His love and kindness. You might also take a nature walk and marvel at God's creation. Thank Him for the beauty around you. It's a great way to worship in spirit — connecting with the character of the Creator through His awe-inspiring creation.

Definitions

Admonishing

Giving gentle or earnest advice, guidance, or warnings to someone with the intention of promoting spiritual growth, understanding, or correction.

Holy

Being set apart, sacred, consecrated for a divine purpose. It signifies purity, righteousness, and being devoted to God and His will.

Worship

The act of reverently adoring and giving praise, honor, and devotion to God. It involves expressing gratitude, love, and reverence through prayer, song, rituals, and acts of service.

Scripture Checklist

- [ ] Psalm 96:9
- [ ] John 4:23–24
- [ ] Romans 12:1
- [ ] 1 Corinthians 10:31
- [ ] Galatians 5:22-23
- [ ] Colossians 3:16–17

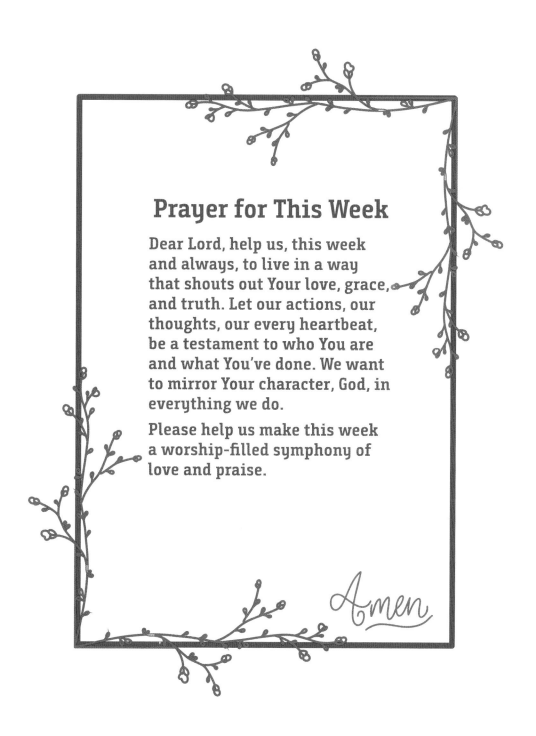

Prayer for This Week

Dear Lord, help us, this week and always, to live in a way that shouts out Your love, grace, and truth. Let our actions, our thoughts, our every heartbeat, be a testament to who You are and what You've done. We want to mirror Your character, God, in everything we do.

Please help us make this week a worship-filled symphony of love and praise.

Amen

49. What is prayer?

Prayer is the persistent (1 Thess. 5:17) pouring out of our hearts to God (Ps. 62:8a), according to God's will (1 John 5:14), with thanksgiving, requests, repentance, worship, and intercession. Prayer is aligning our will with God's will, revealed in His Word, desiring that His kingdom come, and His will be done on earth as it is in heaven.

"Trust in him at all times; ye people, pour out your heart before him."

Psalm 62:8a

"Praying always with all prayer and supplication in the Spirit, and watching thereunto with all perseverance and supplication for all saints."

Ephesians 6:18

"Be careful for nothing; but in every thing by prayer and supplication with thanksgiving let your requests be made known unto God."

Philippians 4:6

"Pray without ceasing."

1 Thessalonians 5:17

"I exhort therefore, that, first of all, supplications, prayers, intercessions, and giving of thanks, be made for all men."

1 Timothy 2:1

"Confess your faults one to another, and pray one for another, that ye may be healed. The effectual fervent prayer of a righteous man availeth much."

James 5:16

"And this is the confidence that we have in him, that, if we ask any thing according to his will, he heareth us."

1 John 5:14

FOUNDATIONAL TRUTH #49
Prayer is aligning our will to God

In Action

This week, make it a morning routine to align your day with God's plan. Take a stroll outside, chat with God about the beauty around you, and align your heart with His creation. As you walk, pray for His will to be done on earth, just like it is in heaven. Grab a notebook and jot down your prayers. Pour out your heart, jot your requests, thank Him, and confess where you've gone wrong. It's like having a written conversation with God.

Definitions

Aligning

The process of bringing one's thoughts, actions, and desires into harmony with God's will, purpose, and teachings.

Effectual

Having a real, significant, and powerful impact or result. It signifies something that is effective, efficient, and productive, often through the work of God or the Holy Spirit.

Thanksgiving

An expression of gratitude and praise to God for His blessings, provisions, and acts of goodness. It's acknowledging and appreciating the gifts and goodness of God with a heart full of thankfulness and joy.

Scripture Checklist

- [ ] Psalm 62:8a
- [ ] Ephesians 6:18
- [ ] Philippians 4:6
- [ ] 1 Thessalonians 5:17
- [ ] 1 Timothy 2:1
- [ ] James 5:16
- [ ] 1 John 5:14

204

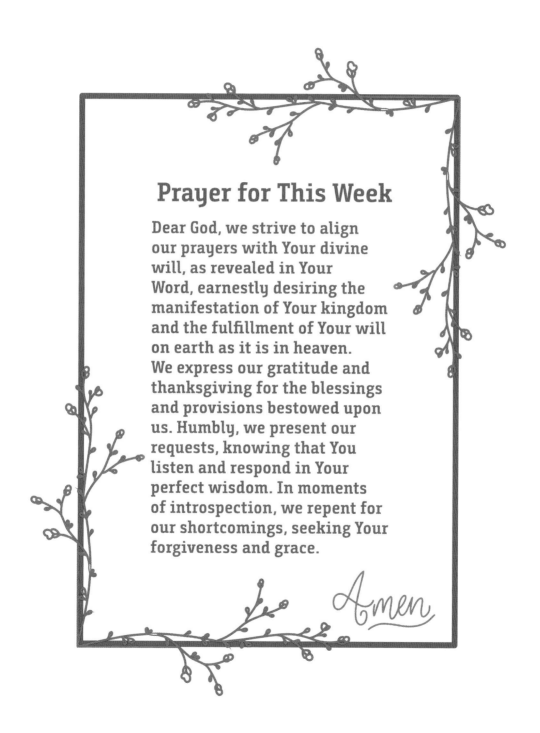

Prayer for This Week

Dear God, we strive to align our prayers with Your divine will, as revealed in Your Word, earnestly desiring the manifestation of Your kingdom and the fulfillment of Your will on earth as it is in heaven. We express our gratitude and thanksgiving for the blessings and provisions bestowed upon us. Humbly, we present our requests, knowing that You listen and respond in Your perfect wisdom. In moments of introspection, we repent for our shortcomings, seeking Your forgiveness and grace.

Amen

50. To whom should we pray?

We pray to the Father in the name of the Son (Matt. 6:9; John 15:16, 16:23b), with the help of the Holy Spirit (Rom. 8:26).

"After this manner therefore pray ye: Our Father which art in heaven, Hallowed be thy name."

Matthew 6:9

"Ye have not chosen me, but I have chosen you, and ordained you, that ye should go and bring forth fruit, and that your fruit should remain: that whatsoever ye shall ask of the Father in my name, he may give it you."

John 15:16

"Verily, verily, I say unto you, Whatsoever ye shall ask the Father in my name, he will give it you."

John 16:23b

"Likewise the Spirit also helpeth our infirmities: for we know not what we should pray for as we ought: but the Spirit itself maketh intercession for us with groanings which cannot be uttered."

Romans 8:26

FOUNDATIONAL TRUTH #50
We pray to the Father, Son, and Spirit

In Action

Allocate a designated time in your weekly schedule, preferably in the morning or evening. Within this sanctified time, engage in sincere and heartfelt communication with God. Express your thoughts, aspirations, anxieties, and gratitude openly, letting your heart be humbled before Him. Offer thanksgiving for blessings received and seek His guidance and intervention for challenges faced.

Definitions

Hallowed

Sacred, holy, or revered. It is often used to describe something or someone set apart for divine, consecrated purposes, deserving respect and veneration.

Infirmities

Weaknesses, illnesses, or physical and moral weaknesses. It often refers to vulnerabilities or shortcomings that individuals experience, which they may seek strength and healing from God for.

Ordained

To be officially appointed, authorized, or consecrated for a specific role or purpose, often within a religious or spiritual context.

Scripture Checklist

- ☐ Matthew 6:9
- ☐ John 15:16
- ☐ John 16:23b
- ☐ Romans 8:26

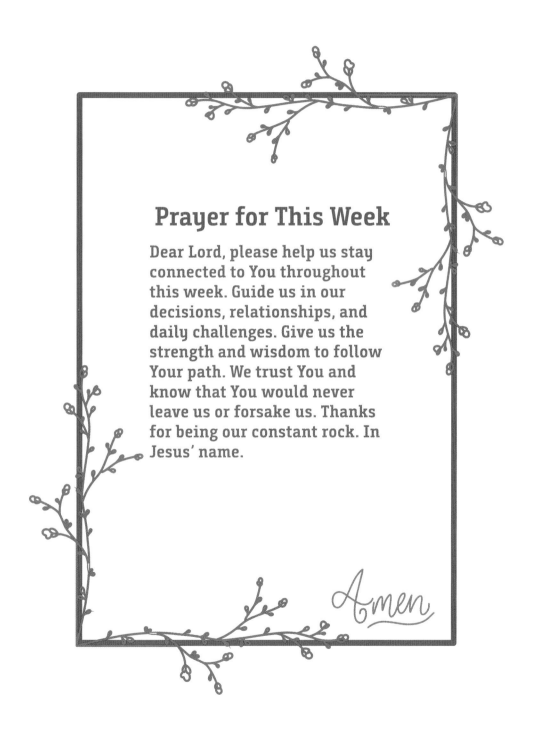

Prayer for This Week

Dear Lord, please help us stay connected to You throughout this week. Guide us in our decisions, relationships, and daily challenges. Give us the strength and wisdom to follow Your path. We trust You and know that You would never leave us or forsake us. Thanks for being our constant rock. In Jesus' name.

Amen

51. Must believers tell others about the gospel of Jesus Christ?

God's followers are commanded to share the truth and hope of salvation through faith in Christ alone to those who are separated from God (2 Cor. 5:20).

"Then saith he unto his disciples, The harvest truly is plenteous, but the labourers are few; Pray ye therefore the Lord of the harvest, that he will send forth labourers into his harvest."

Matthew 9:37–38

"And Jesus came and spake unto them, saying, All power is given unto me in heaven and in earth. Go ye therefore, and teach all nations, baptizing them in the name of the Father, and of the Son, and of the Holy Ghost: Teaching them to observe all things whatsoever I have commanded you: and, lo, I am with you always, even unto the end of the world. Amen."

Matthew 28:18–20

"But ye shall receive power, after that the Holy Ghost is come upon you: and ye shall be witnesses unto me both in Jerusalem, and in all Judaea, and in Samaria, and unto the uttermost part of the earth."

Acts 1:8

"For I am not ashamed of the gospel of Christ: for it is the power of God unto salvation to every one that believeth; to the Jew first, and also to the Greek."

Romans 1:16

"Knowing therefore the terror of the Lord, we persuade men."

2 Corinthians 5:11a

"Now then we are ambassadors for Christ, as though God did beseech you by us: we pray you in Christ's stead, be ye reconciled to God."

2 Corinthians 5:20

"But watch thou in all things, endure afflictions, do the work of an evangelist, make full proof of thy ministry."

2 Timothy 4:5

FOUNDATIONAL TRUTH #51
Believers must share the good news

In Action

This week, make it a goal to chat with someone about your faith journey. Share a bit about what believing in Jesus means to you and how it's impacted your life. Keep it casual and genuine. You never know, it might spark curiosity and open up an opportunity for them to discover the hope you've found in Christ.

Definitions

Ambassadors

People representing or advocating for a higher authority or kingdom, often used to describe Christians representing the teachings and message of Jesus Christ.

Harvest

The gathering of souls, the results of evangelistic efforts where individuals accept and commit to the teachings of Jesus Christ or experience spiritual growth.

Witnesses

Individuals who testify or provide evidence of their faith in Jesus Christ through their words, actions, and lifestyle.

Scripture Checklist

- [ ] Matthew 9:37–38
- [ ] Matthew 28:18–20
- [ ] Acts 1:8
- [ ] Romans 1:16
- [ ] 2 Corinthians 5:11a
- [ ] 2 Corinthians 5:20
- [ ] 2 Timothy 4:5

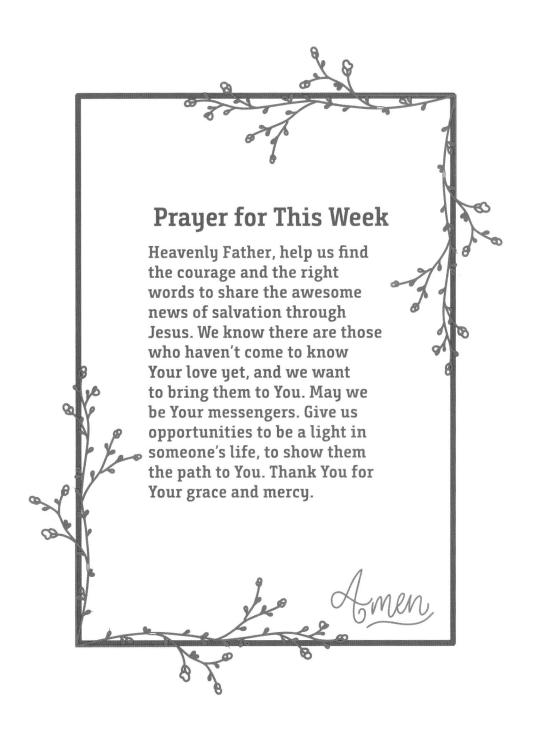

Prayer for This Week

Heavenly Father, help us find the courage and the right words to share the awesome news of salvation through Jesus. We know there are those who haven't come to know Your love yet, and we want to bring them to You. May we be Your messengers. Give us opportunities to be a light in someone's life, to show them the path to You. Thank You for Your grace and mercy.

Amen

52. What is the final destination for Christians in eternity?

We have the promise of eternal life in the presence of God on the New Earth (Rev. 21:1-5).

214

"In my Father's house are many mansions: if it were not so, I would have told you. I go to prepare a place for you. And if I go and prepare a place for you, I will come again, and receive you unto myself; that where I am, there ye may be also."

John 14:2–3

"For he looked for a city which hath foundations, whose builder and maker is God."

Hebrews 11:10

"But now they desire a better country, that is, an heavenly: wherefore God is not ashamed to be called their God: for he hath prepared for them a city."

Hebrews 11:16

"And I saw a new heaven and a new earth: for the first heaven and the first earth were passed away; and there was no more sea. And I John saw the holy city, new Jerusalem, coming down from God out of heaven, prepared as a bride adorned for her husband. And I heard a great voice out of heaven saying, Behold, the tabernacle of God is with men, and he will dwell with them, and they shall be his people, and God himself shall be with them, and be their God. And God shall wipe away all tears from their eyes; and there shall be no more death, neither sorrow, nor crying, neither shall there be any more pain: for the former things are passed away. And he that sat upon the throne said, Behold, I make all things new. And he said unto me, Write: for these words are true and faithful."

Revelation 21:1–5

In Action

Keep this promise of eternal life in your heart as you go about your daily routine. Let it fuel your outlook on life, knowing that whatever you face, there's an amazing future waiting for you with the Lord. Let this promise inspire kindness and generosity. Treat others with love and respect, reflecting the kind of community we hope for one day. Remember, living out this promise is about bringing hope, joy, and love into your life and the lives of those around you.

Definitions

Bride

The representation of the Christian Church as the bride of Christ, symbolizing the intimate and loving relationship between Jesus Christ (the bridegroom) and His followers (the Church).

Faithful

Asserts that what is being conveyed is steadfastly reliable and can be depended upon for accuracy and truthfulness.

Tabernacle

Typically refers to a sacred dwelling place containing consecrated elements dedicated to God's holiness.

Scripture Checklist

- ☐ John 14:2–3
- ☐ Hebrews 11:10
- ☐ Hebrews 11:16
- ☐ Revelation 21:1–5

216

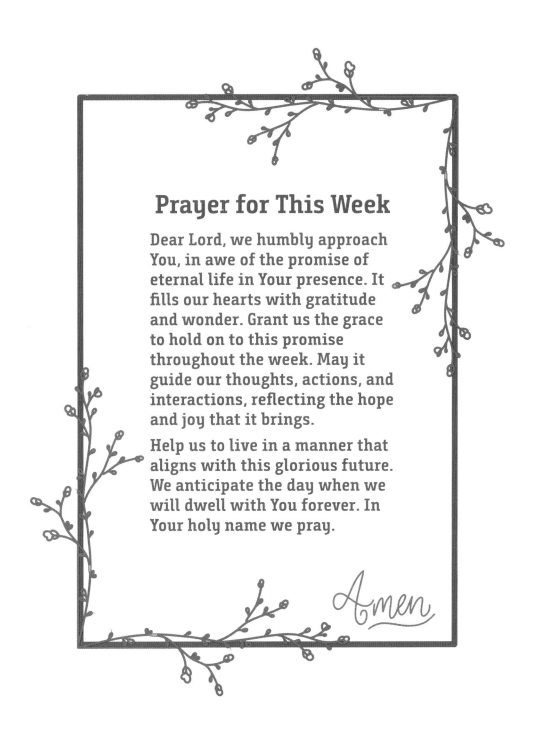

Prayer for This Week

Dear Lord, we humbly approach You, in awe of the promise of eternal life in Your presence. It fills our hearts with gratitude and wonder. Grant us the grace to hold on to this promise throughout the week. May it guide our thoughts, actions, and interactions, reflecting the hope and joy that it brings.

Help us to live in a manner that aligns with this glorious future. We anticipate the day when we will dwell with You forever. In Your holy name we pray.

Amen

What are The 10 Commandments?

 **Thou shalt have none other gods before me.**

2 Thou shalt not make thee any graven image, or any likeness of any thing that is in heaven above, or that is in the earth beneath, or that is in the waters beneath the earth: Thou shalt not bow down thyself unto them, nor serve them: for I the Lord thy God am a jealous God, visiting the iniquity of the fathers upon the children unto the third and fourth generation of them that hate me, And shewing mercy unto thousands of them that love me and keep my commandments.

 **Thou shalt not take the name of the Lord thy God in vain: for the Lord will not hold him guiltless that taketh his name in vain.**

 Keep the sabbath day to sanctify it, as the Lord thy God hath commanded thee. Six days thou shalt labour, and do all thy work: But the seventh day is the sabbath of the Lord thy God: in it thou shalt not do any work, thou, nor thy son, nor thy daughter, nor thy manservant, nor thy maidservant, nor thine ox, nor thine ass, nor any of thy cattle, nor thy stranger that is within thy gates; that thy manservant and thy maidservant may rest as well as thou. And remember that thou wast a servant in the land of Egypt, and that the Lord thy God brought thee out thence through a mighty hand and by a stretched out arm: therefore the Lord thy God commanded thee to keep the sabbath day.

5 Honour thy father and thy mother, as the LORD thy God hath commanded thee; that thy days may be prolonged, and that it may go well with thee, in the land which the Lord thy God giveth thee.

6 Thou shalt not kill.

7 Neither shalt thou commit adultery.

8 Neither shalt thou steal.

9 Neither shalt thou bear false witness against thy neighbour.

10 Neither shalt thou desire thy neighbour's wife, neither shalt thou covet thy neighbour's house, his field, or his manservant, or his maidservant, his ox, or his ass, or any thing that is thy neighbour's.

What is the 23rd Psalm?

The Lord is my shepherd; I shall not want.

He maketh me to lie down in green pastures:
he leadeth me beside the still waters.

He restoreth my soul: he leadeth me in the paths
of righteousness for his name's sake.

Yea, though I walk through the valley of the shadow of death, I will fear
no evil: for thou art with me; thy rod and thy staff they comfort me.

Thou preparest a table before me in the presence of mine enemies:
thou anointest my head with oil; my cup runneth over.

Surely goodness and mercy shall follow me all the days of my life:
and I will dwell in the house of the Lord for ever" (Psalm 23:1–6).

What are "The Beatitudes"?

Blessed are the poor in spirit: for theirs is the kingdom of heaven.

Blessed are they that mourn: for they shall be comforted.

Blessed are the meek: for they shall inherit the earth.

Blessed are they which do hunger and thirst after righteousness: for they shall be filled.

Blessed are the merciful: for they shall obtain mercy.

Blessed are the pure in heart: for they shall see God.

Blessed are the peacemakers: for they shall be called the children of God.

Blessed are they which are persecuted for righteousness' sake: for theirs is the kingdom of heaven.

Blessed are ye, when men shall revile you, and persecute you, and shall say all manner of evil against you falsely, for my sake.

Rejoice, and be exceeding glad: for great is your reward in heaven: for so persecuted they the prophets which were before you (Matthew 5:3–12).

How to Live for God

How to Pray

"And when thou prayest, thou shalt not be as the hypocrites are: for they love to pray standing in the synagogues and in the corners of the streets, that they may be seen of men. Verily I say unto you, They have their reward. But thou, when thou prayest, enter into thy closet, and when thou hast shut thy door, pray to thy Father which is in secret; and thy Father which seeth in secret shall reward thee openly. But when ye pray, use not vain repetitions, as the heathen do: for they think that they shall be heard for their much speaking. Be not ye therefore like unto them: for your Father knoweth what things ye have need of, before ye ask him" (Matthew 6:5–8).

The Lord's Prayer

"After this manner therefore pray ye: Our Father which art in heaven, Hallowed be thy name. Thy kingdom come, Thy will be done in earth, as it is in heaven. Give us this day our daily bread. And forgive us our debts, as we forgive our debtors. And lead us not into temptation, but deliver us from evil: For thine is the kingdom, and the power, and the glory, for ever. Amen" (Matthew 6:9–13).

The Golden Rule

"Therefore all things whatsoever ye would that men should do to you, do ye even so to them: for this is the law and the prophets" (Matthew 7:12).

Fruit of the Spirit

"But the fruit of the Spirit is love, joy, peace, longsuffering, gentleness, goodness, faith, meekness, temperance: against such there is no law" (Galatians 5:22–23).

What is the Nicene Creed?

"I believe in one God, the Father Almighty, Maker of heaven and earth, and of all things visible and invisible.

"And in one Lord Jesus Christ, the only-begotten Son of God, begotten of the Father before all worlds; God of God, Light of Light, very God of very God; begotten, not made, being of one substance with the Father, by whom all things were made.

"Who, for us men for our salvation, came down from heaven, and was incarnate by the Holy Spirit of the virgin Mary, and was made man; and was crucified also for us under Pontius Pilate; He suffered and was buried; and the third day He rose again, according to the Scriptures; and ascended into heaven, and sits on the right hand of the Father; and He shall come again, with glory, to judge the quick and the dead; whose kingdom shall have no end.

"And I believe in the Holy Ghost, the Lord and Giver of Life; who proceeds from the Father [and the Son]; who with the Father and the Son together is worshipped and glorified; who spoke by the prophets.

"And I believe in one holy catholic [universal] and apostolic [based on the teaching of the Apostles] Church. I acknowledge one baptism for the remission of sins; and I look for the resurrection of the dead, and the life of the world to come. Amen."

Scripture Index

FOUNDATIONS IN FAITH

A unique Bible curriculum focused on theology and the foundations of faith. Activities include Bible journaling, exploring church history, and more.

Grade 7–12
978-1-68344-306-3

MASTERBOOKS®
—CURRICULUM—

RAISING THEM UP

Discover the transformative power of parenting as discipleship, rooted in real-world experience and biblical principles.

978-0-89221-765-6

ANSWERS FOR HOMESCHOOLING

Find homeschooling confidence with answers to critical questions in this easy-to-understand book.

978-1-68344-110-6

A BIBLICAL DEFENSE FOR

Homeschooling

IF GOD HAS A
DEFINITE OPINION
ABOUT THE ISSUE OF
EDUCATION,
WOULDN'T YOU
DESIRE TO FIND OUT
WHAT IT IS AND HOW
BEST TO IMPLEMENT
HIS WISDOM?